SHOPPING THE TWIN CITIES
...and more

by

ALISON O'CONNELL

with

Ted May

CHAMBERLIN PUBLISHING
3300 Edinborough Way
Suite 700
Edina, MN 55435

Copyright © 1992 by Chamberlin Publishing.

All rights reserved. No part of this book may be reproduced in any form without written permission from the publisher.

Printed in the United States of America

ISBN 0-9631192-0-6

Published by   Chamberlin Publishing
                    3300 Edinborough Way
                    Suite 700
                    Edina, MN 55435

Typesetting by Carol McPherson, TYPING-TO-GO, 5270 Main Street, Maple Plain, MN 55359

Wallpaper on cover is Payne #04658 "Cherie/African Violet" and is available by special order only. Used by permission.

TABLE OF CONTENTS

INTRODUCTION i

HOW TO USE THIS BOOK ii

ON YOUR MARK 1

DOWNTOWN MINNEAPOLIS
    and WAREHOUSE DISTRICT 7

DOWNTOWN ST. PAUL and GRAND AVENUE 55

UPTOWN 75

EDINA 85
    44th & France 86
    50th & France 86
    Southdale 95
    Galleria 96

LAKE MINNETONKA 115
    Wayzata 115
    Deephaven 134
    Excelsior 137

ART GALLERIES/MUSEUMS 147

ANTIQUE SHOPS 151

CLOTHING CONSIGNMENT SHOPS 171

TABLE OF CONTENTS

OFF THE BEATEN PATH SHOPS 175

SERVICES 199

BY APPOINTMENT ONLY 211

DAY TRIPS: STILLWATER/AFTON 217
               HASTINGS/REDWING 231

TWIN CITY SHOPPING MALLS 243

ABOUT THE AUTHORS 245

SHOPS BY LOCATION 248

SHOPS BY STORE/SERVICE TYPE 259

ALPHABETICAL INDEX 271

ORDER FORM 282

INTRODUCTION

SHOPPING THE TWIN CITIES . . . and more will help you to gain extra value for your money. You will benefit from my experience and research gained over many years of shopping. My first trip to Tiffany's with my father was an initiation into the retail world and the beginning of an adventure that I continue today. I've gained friends in shops around the world and have benefited from their merchandising know-how. Through reading this book you will gain a valuable perspective on the marketplace which will help you choose carefully, spend wisely and live well. Always temper your zest for shopping with a passion for thrift and join me for a tour through some of the most fascinating retail stores you will find anywhere.

The stores, services and restaurants included in this guide were chosen for their potential for quality and value. No financial contributions were received from any businesses listed in this publication. You will sometimes seek the exotic and expensive, sometimes the quaint and the casual but always you will search for value and style at the best prices. You are about to begin, with the assistance of SHOPPING THE TWIN CITIES . . . and more, a serious study of the wonderful retail market of Minneapolis/St. Paul.

SHOPPING THE TWIN CITIES . . . and more is a buyer's guide for the 1990's. Today's consumers should make the best use of their resources. Knowing how and where to shop is the key. This book will take you to the right places and maximize your buying power.

Alison O'Connell

HOW TO USE THIS BOOK

In <u>SHOPPING</u> <u>THE</u> <u>TWIN</u> <u>CITIES</u> . . . <u>and</u> <u>more</u> you will visit several different neighborhoods and will see establishments grouped by area, not by store or merchandise type.

A cross-referenced index in the back of the book lists stores and services by area, by type and alphabetically.

We have taken you to visit the major Twin Cities areas. In addition, we couldn't resist visits to such lovely spots as Stillwater/Afton and Hastings/Red Wing, both great day trip destinations.

We have had a good time writing this book and you'll have a good time reading it.

Break those recession blues and run -- don't walk -- to the stores!

ON YOUR MARK . . .

ON YOUR MARK . . .

It's a jungle out there and to bag the best buys you need an advantage. Prepare for shopping by planning and organizing. Knowing weather conditions, special happenings, bargains and sales, ticket opportunities, store locations and parking availability will lighten the load and make the effort an event. The following are sources of information and assistance that will keep you in touch with the Twin Cities.

WCCO-AM Radio
830 on your dial

The grand potentate of the local airwaves and winner of many awards, WCCO consistently holds the biggest share of the national market. Its broadcasters are simultaneously Minnesotan's best friends and foremost celebrities. Their frivolity and folksiness do not stand in the way of delivering hard news, open minded analysis and critical commentary. 'CCO attracts listeners of all ages and lifestyles in a wide-ranging, around-the-clock format. They have helped write the history of the state and whether it be traffic information or the latest breaking event, the folks at 830 have conquered the market.

Minnesota Public Radio

A state-wide network of 22 public radio stations, this member-supported station has an international reputation for providing first-class music, up-to-date news and thought-provoking analysis. Broadcasting classical music on KSJN (99.5 FM) and news on KNOW (91.1 FM), Minnesota Public Radio brings its listeners a wide range of programming from breaking news events to live musical performances. Minnesota Public Radio is a creative entertainment and news source that invigorates the lives of Minnesotans.

Mpls St. Paul Magazine is published monthly and is the official playbill for metro area people and events. Calendars and schedules, critiques and interviews, human interest stories and slick ad copy make Mpls St. Paul both timely and entertaining. The quality of writing and photography make the publication both friendly and sophisticated.

MINNESOTA TAX INFORMATION

Minnesota Sales Tax is 6.5%, except in Downtown Minneapolis, where it is 7%.

Wearing apparel, prescription drugs and food (as long as it's not prepared, i.e. deli, restaurants, etc. food) are <u>not</u> taxed in Minnesota.

Ticketmaster
989-5151

For tickets to just about any event in the area Ticketmaster is the source.

They do <u>not</u> handle tickets for:

The Guthrie Theater	377-2224
Orchestra Hall	371-5656
Ordway Music Theatre	224-4222

Seat Yourself, providing seating charts for Twin cities auditoriums, legitimate theaters and arenas, is a handy guide (available at book stores) to have when making ticket purchases.

The Connection
922-9000

The Electronic Yellow Pages. A listing service providing business locations and services information, details of public events and the like.

Time of Day	546-TIME
Weather	452-2323

6

DOWNTOWN MINNEAPOLIS
Zip Code 55402

"Lively, active, breathing" are the words used to describe downtown Minneapolis in 1991 by Neiman Marcus president Terry Lundgren. Centered on the Nicollet Mall, the downtown retail scene is friendly and sophisticated. Movement from store to store is enhanced by a skyway system that connects over 3 million square feet of retail space where an estimated 200,000 people traverse daily. The picturesque Mall is the common space that brings together shoppers in downtown Minneapolis. Lining Nicollet are stores that attract millions of people annually. Most prominent among them are Dayton Hudson, Neiman Marcus, Saks Fifth Avenue, Polo Ralph Lauren, Carson Pirie Scott, Brooks Brothers and Burberry's.

People are the main attraction in downtown Minneapolis. The best places to meet or to meander are City Center, the IDS Crystal Court, the Conservatory and Gaviidae Common. The surroundings are stimulating and the people watching is the best in Minnesota.

**Minneapolis Public Library and Planetarium
and Minneapolis Public Library Friends Shop**
300 Nicollet Mall
Minneapolis 55401
372-6500

You can take home more than just books and periodicals from the central branch of the Minneapolis Library. The Planetarium will show you the wonders of the universe. Mylar sunglasses that enable direct viewing of the sun and other science and art gadgets and games are sold in the Planetarium Shop. New and used books attract bibliophiles and smart shoppers to the Friends Shop. Used book prices from 25¢ to $1.00 are a great bargain.

Dome Souvenirs Plus
406 Chicago Avenue
375-9707

Souvenirs from all Minnesota professional sports teams that compete in the Metrodome and a large inventory of baseball cards makes this store a sport lovers' paradise. Collegiate sports clothing and artifacts also available.

Juster's
500 Nicollet Mall
Minneapolis
333-1431

When Harry and P.B. Juster founded Juster Brothers they were the last word in fashion in downtown Minneapolis. The company has expanded and diversified, but Juster's remains the anchor of the men's fashion market. Offering mostly private label for men and women, they take a fastidious approach to providing the right look. Their sense of style allows them to update frequently and infuse both trend and color liberally into their merchandise. Their four Minneapolis locations have become a comfortable home to customers who like the old but wish to experiment with the new in fashion.

10

GAVIIDAE COMMON
5th to 7th Streets on Nicollet Mall
372-1222

There is nothing common about Gaviidae. From its word origin, (Gaviidae is Latin for Loon, the Minnesota state bird) to its upward flowing water fountain (the only one in the world) to its upscale shopping and dining choices (Saks Fifth Avenue, Neiman Marcus, Azur, Toulouse), Gaviidae is one of the wonders of downtown Minneapolis. Since opening in 1989, Gaviidae Common has become a major tourist attraction as well as the site of the metro area's most elaborate merchandising effort. Covering two blocks, Gaviidae has achieved its goal of drawing people into downtown and has had a spectacular impact on the retail scene.

The Saks Fifth Avenue wing of Gaviidae and the Neiman Marcus wing are joined by the "Loon Bridge" which is the only fourth floor skyway in Minneapolis. Designed as an abstract version of the state bird, the bridge features two spreading wings to connect the buildings. There is also a skyway on the second floor.

The spectacular Gaviidae setting is the backdrop for 45 shops featuring the most distinctive apparel, accessories and amenities of contemporary life. Gaviidae shops tend to be pricey although there is a variety of merchandise and there are regular sales in most stores. The two largest stores in the complex, Saks Fifth Avenue and Neiman Marcus, feature prestigious world designers as well as off-the-rack items to accommodate their varied clientele.

Gaviidae offers comforts that can lessen the rigors of shopping. Valet parking under both wings, car wash (by hand and by appointment -- 372-1620 for 6th Street garage, 343-2112 for 5th Street garage), wheelchairs and strollers, and choice dining make the experience of shopping at Gaviidae pleasant.

The prize of Gaviidae restaurants is Azur, the fifth floor celebration of French cuisine. Toulouse is a cafeteria-style restaurant also offering French foods. Morton's Steakhouse is a branch of the famous Chicago restaurant. For a quick bite, there is Grandma Gebhards and Annie's Frozen Yogurt. A unique convenience store, Solostop, has health and beauty aids, candy, cigarettes, dry cleaning and fax services.

NEIMAN MARCUS WING

Neiman Marcus
505 Nicollet Mall
339-2600

Neiman Marcus is a piece of our national heritage. Everything they touch sparkles with style and elan. It consistently ranks at the top of the national market and sets an industry standard for excellence in merchandise and marketing. Their annual Christmas catalog, famous for its fantasy gifts, adorns coffee tables long after the season is over. The Minneapolis store has it all -- from the show-stopping gift galleries and men's department on the street level to luggage, women's exquisite hats, gloves, bags, shoes, jewelry and cosmetics on the Skyway level to lingerie, coats and sportswear on three and furs, couture and evening wear, defining the truly elegant woman, on four. An exciting new addition to Neiman Marcus is an A/X Armani Exchange shop which carries a collection of jeans and casual clothes for men and women under the Armani jeans label.

Neiman Marcus' commitment to customer service is headlined by the concierge who will check your coat, provide store information, give directions, arrange for package delivery, open a credit account, call a cab, make dining reservations or attend to any other customer concern. Plans include an in-store restaurant.

Gregory's
338-5388

This high-test shoe store from Dallas offers the best names in women's footwear. Petra, Stuart Weitzman, Charles David, Pancaldi, Modigliani, Via Spiga all set the stage for a good local showing of Europe's finest shoes.

Urban Traveler
341-4001

Made for people who are on the go, Urban Traveler has bags, travel accessories, briefcases and gift items of high quality. Top-notch in style and construction, Andiamo luggage is featured here. Traveling can be a hassle unless you are well prepared. A stop at Urban Traveler should be the first leg of any journey. There are Urban Traveler shops at Calhoun Square (822-6726), Galleria (922-3672) and in Roseville (631-9655).

---

* * * * * * * *

Morton's of Chicago
673-9700

Known for its 24-ounce steaks and 1-pound baked potatoes, Morton's is definitely an adult place to eat. Add to that the Frank Sinatra music, paneled bar and sturdy elegance and Morton's is a durable and memorable eating experience.

* * * * * * * *

SAKS FIFTH AVENUE WING

Saks Fifth Avenue
333-7200

Saks Fifth Avenue is a nationally known retailer representing quality merchandise and exceptional service, specializing in the best of the world's designer and fashion accessories for men and women.

The personalized services of the 5th Avenue Club and One on One provide customer shopping to fit individual needs. Consultants assist with advice on the newest trends, determine preferences and assess wardrobe requirements. They may also preselect merchandise for approval, or arrange a tour of the store.

However you like to shop, Saks Fifth Avenue offers a wide range of products from classic to contemporary for career and casual lifestyles including unique jewelry and Estate Collections, Salon Z for full figures, Petites, Layette and Infants, SFA Logo apparel and foods, Cafe SFA, and the Beauty Salon.

Saks Fifth Avenue, the ultimate shopping experience.

Olds Pendleton Shop
340-0771

The Pendleton line of classic woolen fabric, blankets, men's and women's sportswear is known for its style and durability. This shop is a complete source of this American-made look. A Pendleton will last you a lifetime and can be a legacy for the next generation.

j. mcgrath & co.
339-3757

This unique store has gorgeous one-of-a-kind jewelry and home accessories ranging from the functional to the merely decorative. There are creations by recognized designers that make j. mcgrath a place for gifts and personal buying unmatched in the Twin Cities.

The Lenox China Store
338-3000

The seemingly endless array of Lenox, Gorham and Dansk pieces in dignified traditional or upscale modern fill this enchanting store. China, dinnerware, stemware, pewter, sterling, figurines, corporate gift service and bridal registry. The Lenox look is a good one and their periodic sales make it that much more attractive.

Barrie Pace Ltd.
338-8288

Wardrobe consultation and shopping-by-appointment make Barrie Pace ideal for the busy woman. They feature the tailored look for active, stylish businesswomen. Their in-store tailors assure that customers will look right. Barrie Pace is part of Liemandt's, the respected men's clothier. Also at Galleria (927-4558).

Burberrys of London
333-3600

The creators of the classic trench coat offer traditional and updated apparel for men and women. With shops in London, Paris and New York, "the Burburry look" represents the very finest in styling and materials. Their personalized service and tailoring allows their well known and easily recognizable style to look new and distinct on each customer.

Cole-Haan
339-4662

Fine footwear and leather goods for men, women and children (ages 7 and older). Plaid umbrellas, popular woven leather handbags, great men's socks. Cole-Haan is simply exquisite in design and material. Through fads and trends, Cole-Haan has maintained a continental flair.

The Icing
338-2693

A kiss on the hand may be quite continental, but The Icing has rhinestones and glitter sufficient enough to answer anyone's most glitzy dreams. Blazers, sweaters and blouses, hats, bags and hair accessories which drip with colors and stones are done with taste. You can bejewel yourself with style at either the Gaviidae or Southdale (925-4376) store.

SKYWAY LEVEL SHOPS

Westminster Lace
332-4120

The look of romantic finery is found at Westminster Lace. Trousseau selections, bed and dining linens, nightgowns and peignoirs, crystal and silver, sachets, pot pourri, handkerchiefs and hats are done beautifully.

The San Francisco Music Box Company
332-4248

Wall to wall, floor to ceiling, music boxes at all price levels fill this spectacular shop. Every theme, mood or occasion has a song that is expressed in one of their hundreds of boxes. Snow globes, figurines, carrousels, clowns and dolls complete this sonorous shopping experience.

Eddie Bauer
339-9477

Assured, warm, cozy, sturdy, natural -- this is the reputation of Eddie Bauer. Denim, down, flannel, wool and cotton. Their well-priced outdoor and casual clothing has been outfitting women, men and children for more than 70 years. There are seven metro area locations.

First Issue
338-3436

Liz Claiborne's First Issue offers mix and match sportswear for a fast paced world. Their renditions of her look meet the needs of the working woman who enjoys an active life.

The Museum Company
339-3370

They teach a little history with each purchase. The Museum Company sells authorized replicas of priceless art, much in the manner of the Metropolitan Museum of Art gift shop. Their stock includes copies of ancient sculpture and statuary, reproductions of paintings, jewelry, china, curios and glassware. Dress your purchases in their unique wrapping paper and choose a card with a Matisse or Picasso motif. The Museum Company makes the rare and exotic attainable at reasonable prices.

Sans Souci Leather & Luggage
375-9566

These are high class, timeless leather goods. Luggage, handbags, business card cases, briefcases, attaches are in the very best of taste and the very best of quality. The Sans Souci reputation is one of the few that speaks entirely for itself.

3RD LEVEL SHOPS

Anne Klein
371-9622

For that distinctive Anne Klein look, this shop can fill your every wish. Carrying A-Line, Anne Klein II and Anne Klein III as well as jewelry, scarves, belts and footwear.

Cache
338-0461

Friendly shop assistants will lead you through a brightly lit parade of baubles, bangles and beads. Jeweled hats, blouses, jackets, slacks and evening wear that will make any occasion a memorable one are the order of the day at Cache. Their Vogue fashions are quite stunning!

Laurel
340-1300

Fabulous fabrics and daring designs make Laurel one of the top women's fashion merchandisers in the area. Laurel is an offspring of Escada USA and is known for statement blouses and important dresses emblazoned with embroidered crests in wonderful colors. The jazzy Crisca line is also available here.

Brentano's Book Store
338-6808

This collection of best seller, classic and specialized books is a reliable source for the reader and the bearer of gifts. The staff knows the book market -- they are able to advise customers about what's new and what's old in the trade.

H2O Plus
341-3355

The floor-to-ceiling glass exterior of H2O Plus gives the message that this place is neat, clean and shiny in all that it does. Reasonable prices and easy application of gels, soaps, lotions and creams for the body are the stock and trade of this fast moving company. The pure and simple approach to health and beauty has strong appeal in a busy society.

Jessica McClintock, Inc.
338-7832

Romantic, sweet, old-fashioned styles for girls and women, all decked out in lace, velvet and satin. This precious look is ideal for Easter, prom and weddings. McClintock dexterously balances Pollyanna with a contemporary appeal. Shoes and accessories complete the ensembles. Also available are Scott McClintock frocks, which are less expensive, and the Gunne Sax line for girls to junior sizes.

Rodier Paris
339-8575

This place knows its stuff. Founder Jacques Rodier was once a weaver for Chanel. Rodier offers an extensive collection of timeless traditional knits in vibrant colors with accessories that enliven and enhance the classic. This is for the truly fashionable woman.

Lillie Rubin
332-4210

Lillie Rubin has earned its wild and wonderful reputation in the women's clothing market. It is the wardrobe department for many television stars and also provides duds for anyone wanting trendy clothes ornamented with sequins, pearls, studs, stones, leather inserts and sophisticated charm.

Baxter's Books
608 - 2nd Avenue South
Minneapolis 55402
339-4922

This is what a book store should be. Cozy and inviting, Baxter's asks visitors to approach matters of the mind and the senses as a natural part of everyday life. This is what a book should do. Baxter's stimulates people to pursue their interests and improve their lives through reading. It's an entirely civil refuge in the hectic downtown scene. They frequently host author signings including the recent appearance of Robert K. Massie, author of <u>Dreadnought</u>.

The Map Store
120 South 6th Street
Minneapolis 55402
339-4117

From the downtown skyway system to the world, The Map Store will show you where to go. The metro area's largest selection of atlases, globes, maps and map accessories is found here. If you plan to visit London, Paris or Topeka, prepare for your trip by getting to know the city. Fun items such as lake shirts from Minnesota and the Great Lakes, interesting puzzles and the paraphernalia of travel add to the fascinating world scene you can get here. Also St. Paul (227-6277).

Hubert W. White
611 Marquette Avenue
Minneapolis 55402
339-9200

If you make good money and have good taste, go no further than Hubert W. White. Their lines include E & J Pake, Nick Hilton, Norman Hilton and Oxxford. You will feel good about yourself, your style and your money will be well spent in this classy shop.

Carson Pirie Scott
600 On The Mall
347-7611

A friendly counterpoint to its neighbor across the street, Carson's enjoys the loyalty of customers from its predecessor, the venerable Donaldson's. The downtown store flares with color and is a respected team player with its competitors on the Nicollet Mall. A multi-category department store that opens onto the City Center, Carson's airy, upscale atmosphere offers the reasonable shopping alternative. Its women's hat department is worth a visit.

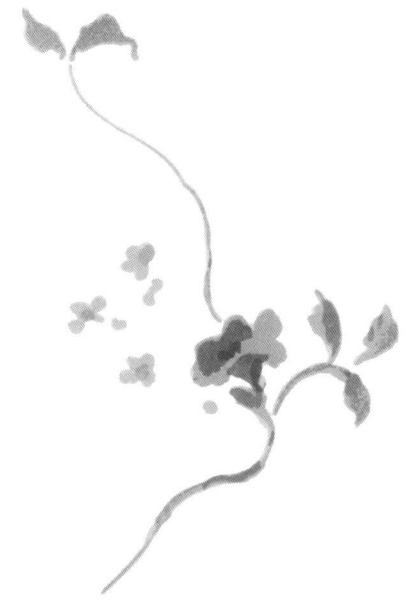

CITY CENTER
33 South 7th Street
372-1234

City Center is the "great room" of downtown Minneapolis. This gathering spot for shoppers, tourists, locals and people watchers is open, expansive and inviting. In City Center you will see the urban mix in every dimension and color. Piano concerts on the first floor echo throughout the Center and there's rush and excitement on all three floors.

Here you'll find several shops that have many Twin Cities locations. The mushrooming **Limited** (375-1093) is here, as is its **Express** (339-3843) with casual clothing -- rompers, jumpsuits, tanks, T-shirts and trousers, all with a European air. **Victoria's Secret** (375-1024) has lingerie, beautiful picture frames, bath goods in yummy fragrances such as peach and hyacinth. **Lane Bryant** (338-8163) has casual, career and evening wear for the larger woman.

The latest in athletic footwear is available at the **Foot Locker** (333-5573) and denim of all descriptions is at the **County Seat** (338-6635). Norwegian "Hearts and Pines" china and Royal Copenhagen porcelains adorn **Scandia Imports** (339-6339). **Laura Ashley** (332-6066) has dresses and separates, wallpaper, lampshades, perfumes and accessories all covered with the tiny flowers of Laura Ashley's famous prints.

Hoffritz (339-0229) offers cutlery and gadgets galore. **Gantos** (332-3490) sports jeweled T-shirts, jumpsuits, hats, handbags, gloves, belts and fashion jewelry. They have lots of denim, good bathing suits and coats. **Aeropostale** (341-0464) is a division of Macy's and the first of its kind in Minnesota. What the jungle is to **Banana Republic**, the airplane hangar is to Aeropostale. The store is full of steel drums, metal shelving, wooden crates and Mobil gasoline signs which serve as props to display army-colored casual clothing, backpacks and blankets. **Mother's Work** (339-0150) is a nice maternity shop with career, casual and evening choices. Not everyone is a size 10 so **Petite Sophisticate** (338-6502) caters to the smaller woman. City Center also has a **B. Dalton Bookstore** (332-8363) and **Bachman's** (333-3450). At **Gloria Jean's** (332-0688) you'll see the largest assortment of coffees, coffee makers and accessories this side of Brazil.

The top level Food Hall houses just about every kind of fast food in America from McDonald's to Grandma's Cookies. There is plentiful seating in a clean, well-lit area which is a gathering spot for shoppers and the younger set.

Dayton's
700 On The Mall
375-2200

What can you say about Dayton's? It's Helen Hayes' favorite place to buy coats, it towers above its competitors and it is a national merchandising phenomenon. Built on the original site of Westminster Presbyterian Church, the anchor store at 7th and Nicollet is at the apex of the downtown retail market. What distinguishes Dayton's from the rest is an 89-year-old record of selling and servicing the Twin City area. Their strategies are the most up-to-date merchandise, a no-questions-asked return policy and killer sales. Whether indulging in Oval Room splendor, dining in the 12th floor Oak Grill or selecting from their enormous spectrum of goods and services, Dayton's has value and ambiance everywhere.

Dayton's Furniture and Design Studio is the most elegant living room in Minneapolis. This massive collection of European, American and Oriental pieces is arranged in room settings that carry out theme and mood in stunning detail. Designers will assist in planning your rooms and selecting appointments. Their motto is customer preference so you can make your own statement. Dayton's is one of the area's best sources of Oriental carpets. Kitchen appliances and design consultation are available.

Life is a banquet and no one need want as long as Dayton's Marketplace is in business. This is a bazaar of international flavors. Amid ready to eat salads, pasta, meats, cheeses, pastries and specialty fare, there is satisfaction for every palate.

Fine caviar, smoked salmon and foie gras are presented in tempting display. For under a dollar you can have gourmet cheese and bread or for just $86.00 you may treat yourself to Beluga caviar. Showcase after showcase bulging with snack-time treats and haute cuisine makes Marketplace a prime watering hole for shoppers.

J. B. Hudson Jewelers
770 Nicollet Mall
338-5950
Southdale, Ridgedale, Burnsville, Brookdale, St. Paul

Made for a king, fit for a commoner, J. B. Hudson Jewelers has been selling treasures to Minneapolitans since 1886. The downtown Minneapolis store is simply elegant and speaks of an era when intricate grillwork, marble arches and crystal chandeliers greeted liveried shoppers arriving on Nicollet Avenue. Hudson's is the local agent for the world's most magnificent estate pieces, contemporary classics, custom-made designs, fine gifts and timepieces including Cartier and Rolex. They deal in the highest quality gems and jewels with superb craftsmanship. J. B. Hudson Jewelers provides pleasures for generations and is a showpiece of the local retail market.

Radisson Hotel, Plaza VII
45 South 7th Street

Facets
375-0554

Styled after a European salon, Facets features designer jewelry, genuine gems and one-of-a-kind pieces that will give a lifetime of pleasure. Watches include Chopard and Rolex and this upscale jewel of a shop displays Baccarat crystal among the diamonds. Parking validated in hotel.

Christensen Mix Ltd.
338-4056

Contemporary, colorful clothing. A store for the self-confident and courageous man. Christensen Mix dares to be different and is always one step ahead of others. One of the biggest and boldest tie selections in town.

THE CONSERVATORY
800 Nicollet Mall
332-4649

The marble walls and winding staircases, abundant greenery and upscale retailers of The Conservatory add a touch of distinctive shopping to the Twin Cities. One of the newest entrants to the competitive downtown market, The Conservatory is slick and stunning and has shops that are not found in other Twin City shopping centers.

Complements at the Conservatory
339-0884

One-of-kind costume jewelry pieces, scarves, belts, handbags and hats have been selected with an eye for the very contemporary woman. Their gift wrappings have the splendor of luminous foil and twinkling stars.

Jean Stephen Galleries
338-4333

Goofy, Mickey, Bugs - the gang welcomes you to the first of two locations. In the first floor Gallery are limited edition cartoon celluloids. The interesting details and characteristic expressions of the cinematic heroes are genuine collectors' items. Up on the fourth floor Jean Stephen has investment grade contemporary original and limited edition art. This gallery holds some of the liveliest and most expressive works available anywhere.

Crabtree & Evelyn
339-2155

Bathe yourself in luxury and give your body the attention it deserves. English sachets, soaps, shampoos, body lotions, combs and brushes. Many items are available in keepsake hat boxes or patterned tins. The wide variety of goods provides a lift for every budget.

Doubleday Book Shop
338-5700

Doubleday's national reputation for providing the best, the latest and the most complete selection of books is maintained in their small Twin Cities store. The skills of the industry's best marketers and insights into readers' lives give Doubleday an edge on the book world that continually makes them a source of fascinating and varied material.

The Nature Company
339-1510

As arresting and diverse as nature itself, The Nature Company is for people who appreciate nature and want to explore its wonders. From the mood lighting to the recorded sounds, when entering The Nature Company, you become more aware of your environment. Telescopes, microscopes, binoculars, fossil specimens, small animal sculptures, children's toys, posters, books, wind chimes, jewelry, art pieces and gifts. From its simple to its exotic elements, this is a tribute to the beauty of the earth.

Mark Shale
334-3323

Clothes for the young professional man and woman in the foremost designer names. Their selection of ties is massive and spectacular. Mark Shale is a comprehensive clothier known for personal attention and wardrobe consultation.

Pottery Barn
338-1654

Not just a barn, not just pottery, this shop has an eclectic selection of tableware, rugs, candles and candle holders, Bavarian glass ornaments, chili pepper lights, gift wrapping paper, vases, potpourri, do-it-yourself decorating materials, and things that cannot be imagined, such as a Wild West muffin pan. Prices are low to reasonable. Four elegant gemstone mugs sell for $20.

The Sharper Image
338-8610

If you want a glimpse of the next century, stop at The Sharper Image. The good life through technology is their pitch and they have a seemingly endless supply of new ideas. This company is on the cutting edge of what's new in the world of scientific and technological development for the consumer. All merchandise is intended to make life easier and healthier. Lounge chairs that are equipped with vibration and sound, exercise equipment, leather jackets, stereophonic equipment, gadgets and tools of life in the 21st Century. The Sharper Image is a museum for the future.

St. Croix Shop
339-0128

This shop has a fascination with color. The most popular item is the short sleeved cotton lisle shirt available in 17 hues. Upper bracket jackets, sweaters, shirts and socks for men are wisely selected and beautifully displayed. Countess Mara and St. Croix labels spell a crisp and vivid appearance.

* * * * * * * * *

Tejas
375-0800 Restaurant
375-1132 Take Out

For a break and refueling during a shopping excursion, Tejas provides Southwestern cuisine that is exotic, colorful and intense with taste. They also have take-out.

* * * * * * * * *

Ann Taylor
338-4308

Classic styling for the young executive set is the theme of Ann Taylor. Lots of "little black dresses" that are suitable for the office by day and, with a string of pearls, are easily transformed into a dinner dress. Shoes, bags, jewelry in styles and designs that convey confidence. Also at Southdale (922-6868) and Ridgedale (593-9842)

The Coach Store
333-1772

All over the country the Coach label is a sign of good taste and long wear. Handcrafted natural leathergoods including jotters, key cases, wallets, cashmere lined gloves, handbags, braces, belts, folios, diaries, organizers for seemingly everything and weather-resistant lightweight luggage all have the famous Coach look.

Gap Kids
339-2303

Other than the major department stores, Gap Kids is the only place downtown to buy children's clothing. The fare is just plain cute in its traditional, preppy, school-kid look. The colors are flattering kids' colors and the fabrics and designs promise durability. There are Gap Kids outlets at Ridgedale (591-9833), Southdale (922-3818), and Burnsville (898-1100). The Southdale store also has Baby Gap.

Banana Republic
333-6323

The safari look comes to the city. Chambray shirts, khaki pants, plaid shirts, wool sweaters, cotton shorts and T-shirts, hats and accessories are the order of the day. More substantial wear includes rugged leather jackets and wool blazers. Occasionally you'll see fun, flowered travel bags. There are Banana Republic stores at Southdale (922-5070) and Ridgedale (525-0595).

Williams-Sonoma
370-0086

Gadgets and gizmos with utility and panache are at Williams-Sonoma. From country charm to urban sophistication, all styles of housewares are represented. French vineyard placemats and crystal stemware, Kitchen Aid mixers and ethnic cookbooks are found amid the biggest and most colorful kitchen and housewares collection around town. Whether gourmet or beginner, Williams-Sonoma has thought of its audience and put together just about everything a kitchen needs. Their products are also available in the Galleria (925-0039).

Call of the Wild
341-3467

In this authentic log cabin setting, there is clothing by Woolrich, blankets, gift and decorative items that reflect life in Minnesota and the great outdoors. The medium is the message here and it is pure good life. Also in Eden Prairie Center (942-7595) and Roseville (636-2141).

FAO Schwarz
339-2233

Every child's dreams come true at FAO Schwarz. This satellite of the famous New York store has enormous stuffed animals, life-like dolls, trucks, cars and trains resplendent in technological detail, games and puzzles enough for the better-than-average whiz kid and an endless serving of wonder and fantasy. The special magic of childhood is conveyed in every piece at FAO Schwarz. A trip through this store is a journey to a land where life is carefree and everything is possible. It beckons children of every generation.

* * * * * * * * *

Goodfellows
332-4800

Take time to savor the classy elegance of Goodfellows. Their fancy fare is meant to be enjoyed. Not a place to stop while on the run, but a first class dining experience where you'll want to take time to savor every delicious bite.

* * * * * * * * *

LASALLE COURT
8th Street and LaSalle

In the hub of the downtown retail market, LaSalle Court is a link between the Conservatory, Dayton's and LaSalle Plaza. Although there are only a handful of retail shops in LaSalle Court, it is one of the busiest spots downtown. Shoppers and workers pass through daily making the Court a prime place for watching people. The limited number of clothing stores are well established members of the retail community and feature an inventory of quality goods.

Sims
333-5275

Tailored to a "T" and secure in its traditional presence, Sims has a solid reputation in men's clothing circles in the Twin Cities. Featuring business wear and custom made suits, their labels include Norman Hilton and Alexander Julian, Nautica sportswear and shoes by Mephisto. They also have a store in Wayzata (473-4633).

Charles Couture
343-0421

Promoting a look that is daring and has an Italian flair, Charles Couture is a leading downtown clothier. Charles carries suits by Bill Robinson, Lubiam, Jane Barnes and Tomary.

Charles Footwear
332-3011

The Italian look is very much in evidence here although there are many designers and styles sold. They include Cole-Haan, Bally, Kenneth Cole, Charles Jourdan, Zodiac and Rockport. There are over 400 patterns of ties and a giant collection of men's socks including designs by Givenchy and Armani. Also at Calhoun Square (825-1716).

Soldati
332-4597

In one stop you will see the finest in women's contemporary footwear. The best names, the slickest looks, the great leathers are found in the Mephisto, Via Spiga and Anne Klein inventory. Complement your shoes with belts, bags and a whole booty of accessories.

---

* * * * * * * * *

Palomino
LaSalle Plaza
339-3800

The brightest new star in the downtown firmament, Palomino has introduced a lively sophistication to local dining. Billed as a Euro-Metro bistro, the atmosphere is bright, artsy and jocular. Hand-blown glass triumvirate chandeliers and giant Matisse repros set the stage for whirlwind service and an Italian leaning menu. Diners will want to take their time, savoring the experience. (The Tiramisu dessert has been known to cause spontaneous but tasteful outbursts.) Palomino is top shelf.

* * * * * * * * *

Albrecht's
829 Nicollet Mall
Minneapolis 55402
333-8104

Throughout changing times Albrecht's has held sway on the downtown fashion market. Labels such as Dalton, Victor Costa and St. John continue to attract loyal customers and make Albrecht's a source of the good look. They have a corner on the market for the popular, little trunk-shaped handbags in a variety of colors. Their selection of important suits and dresses is accented by dressy and colorful accessories.

Brooks Brothers
IDS Center
Minneapolis
338-6600

Brooks Brothers sells variations on classic themes in men's and women's clothing. They have maintained a national reputation for bringing to the American business community a look that rarely varies from its traditional, self-assured center. For people who see their wardrobes as an investment that will last them into the future, Brooks Brothers has the goods and the style that will open the right doors.

The Polo/Ralph Lauren Shop
9th and Nicollet
338-7000

Located in the most architecturally distinctive building on the Mall, Polo/Ralph Lauren combines working class style and leisurely elegance in a comprehensive assemblage of America's most characteristic fashion look. The feel of country casualness melds with drawing room formality in Lauren's extensive collection of men's, women's and children's clothing and domestic linens and effects. The opulence and spaciousness of the Polo/Ralph Lauren Shop underscores the color, texture and design of their superb collection. Ralph Lauren is a major influence on the American image of the 1990's. The Nicollet Mall store is the second largest of Lauren's family of trend-setting shops throughout the country. Valet parking is validated in the Young Quinlan ramp.

Haskell's and The Big Cheese Company
81 South Ninth Street
Minneapolis 55402
333-2434

The world of wine and liquor can be confusing and costly to both the veteran and the novice. Haskell's has 58 years of experience bringing quality spirits and service to the Twin Cities. The knowledgeable sales staff can advise patrons on the appropriate wine or liquor for any type of entertaining. Haskell's is known for sales that offer premium brands at very good prices. Whether your taste is Dom Perignon or Bud Light, Haskell's will give you what you want. They also have cheeses, sandwiches and salad to take out at this location. Validated parking. Four locations.

Crate and Barrel
915 Nicollet Mall
Minneapolis 55402
338-4000

Whether it be plain or fancy, old home or high tech, juvenile or adult, domestic or foreign, they've got the goods. This great, big, glassed-in warehouse has domestic and decorative merchandise which literally jumps out at shoppers and beckons for a new home. You can count on excellent style and the latest design at Crate and Barrel. They have miles of glassware, pottery, acrylics, porcelains, a spectacular selection of gadgets, bath accessories, patio furniture and planters, marble and wood vases and the kitchen sink.

Pier 1 Imports
904 Nicollet Mall
Minneapolis 55402
341-2838

Pier 1 is a lifeline to the arts and crafts of the world. The romantic white paper lanterns which have lighted homes for two decades are the signature piece of a store that brings butcher block tables from Thailand, dining chairs from Italy, barstools from Indonesia and stemware from Holland. Amid the myriad of accessories and decorations, you will find at Pier 1 the flair and color that only an international market can offer. You can take a trip around the world and never leave home with Pier 1 Imports' lively fare at exceptional savings. Pier 1 has 11 metro area stores.

Eddie Bauer Outlet Store
821 Marquette Avenue
Minneapolis 55402
341-0504

Outerwear, comfort wear, sportswear and solid fashion are the ticket at Eddie Bauer's Foshay Tower Outlet Store. At savings from 30% to 70% on quality casual and sportswear, Eddie Bower is the area's most reliable shop for the well-presented outdoor look. If you ski in the winter or swim and sail in the summer, Bauer can dress you for the active life. There are also five Eddie Bauer retail stores in the area including the neighboring shop in Gaviidae Common.

Judi Designs
1010 Marquette
Minneapolis 55402
332-8445

The big yellow awning is as warm and inviting as the choice stems and bouquets you'll find at Judi Designs. This lovely shop brings a touch of "neighborhood" to downtown. Decorated wreaths, topiaries, fresh flowers and plants are delivered (without charge in the downtown area) reliably. Judi specializes in convention and business trade, but no order is too small and individual attention accompanies every petal.

Flowers On The Mall
920 Nicollet Mall
375-1821

Katie Hanson displays her Oriental skill in designing floral arrangements that are delivered quickly and cheerfully to nearby hotels and office buildings.

Perspectives Fine Arts Gallery
924 Nicollet Mall
Minneapolis 55402
339-6076

A contemporary American crafts gallery where over 100 artists in all medias -- ceramic, wood, glass, fibers, oils, acrylics and jewelry -- display their wares in a varied and dignified collection. Prices are good on very fine pieces of art.

Beard Galleries
1104 Nicollet Mall
332-5592

For more than a century this gallery has presented fine 19th and 20th Century, European and American paintings and prints and the works of established local artists.

Vern Carver Gallery
1106 Nicollet Mall
Minneapolis 55402
339-3449

This is one of the prime sources of retail art in the Twin Cities. Their thorough collection includes original works by the foremost local artists. They also have reproductions of masters' works especially Impressionists and works from the Flemish school. Antique handcolored etchings as well as contemporary posters complete the presentation. Botanicals by Curtis and birds by J. J. Audubon. Their custom framing, done with distinctive hand painted mats, enhances the painting or poster.

* * * * * * * * *

Brit's Pub
1110 Nicollet Mall
Minneapolis
332-3908

Authentic British cuisine on the Nicollet Mall features Scotch Eggs, Shepherd's Pie, Steak and Kidney Pie and London Broil. The bar has a full supply of British ales and spirits, and the decor, complete with a photo of the Queen Mum, sets the stage for a thoroughly enjoyable dining occasion. Your host for breakfast, lunch, high tea or dinner will be Nigel Chilvers who is as English as the menu. This is an upbeat alternative to the usual spots found in the Twin Cities. It is jolly good!

* * * * * * * * *

Orchestra Hall WAMSO Gift Shop
1111 Nicollet Mall
371-5654

The Minnesota Orchestra and a calendar of visiting artists perform in this acoustically perfect hall. The Gift Shop allows concert goers to take home a piece of the evening. Many items appeal directly to music lovers. They include Minnesota Orchestra items, including T-shirts and sweats, ceramic cups decorated with musical notes and composers names, jewelry and toys for adults and children. Operated by the Women's Association of the Minnesota Orchestra (WAMSO), the Gift Shop is open during concerts and also on the Marktplatz during Sommerfest.

Dublin Walk
1200 Nicollet Mall
338-5203

This shop sparkles with everything Ireland exports including crystal, porcelains, knitwear and teatime foods. The friendly shopkeeper can also help you prepare for a trip to Ireland with maps, guide books and tips gained from first-hand experience.

Hello Minnesota
7 South 7th Street
332-1755

1200 Nicollet Mall
339-5996

Mugs, magnets, blankets and clothing featuring the North Star State, plus wild rice, American Indian crafts and exclusive work by Minnesota artists. The loon and the lady slipper are celebrated here in every shape and form. Hello Minnesota sells the cultural heritage of the state in useful and decorative ways, and has since 1974 been known as "The Best Minnesota Store in the World."

HYATT REGENCY HOTEL
1300 Nicollet Mall

Elegance
338-8833

Located on the second level in the Hyatt Regency Hotel, owner Connie Olson presents women's career-oriented clothing with flair. There are accessories and unique sweaters -- plus many items male travelers might forget to pack, such as cuff links and collar stays.

* * * * * * * * *

Manny's
339-9900

A steak house reminiscent of the great New York and Chicago steak houses, Manny's boasts the largest stock of red wines available in five states. "Sirloins, porterhouses, primes, and filets large enough to cause a dislocated shoulder, well-cut, well-aged, and sided with proper he-man (if he's godzilla) trimmings," says the Twin Cities Reader.

* * * * * * * * *

The Douglas-Baker Gallery
332-2978

This gallery features figurative, landscape and architectural paintings from classic to abstract. Privately owned by Doug Koons, Douglas-Baker presents unique beaded African jewelry alongside decorative arts and prisms from 20th Century jewelers. Always open by appointment in addition to regular hours.

Shinder's
733 Hennepin Avenue
333-3628

From the Sydney Morning Herald to the Decorah Posten, Shinder's brings the world to Minneapolis. It houses a large collection of foreign journals, regional gazettes, collector magazines and comics. Catering to the diverse and the depraved, Shinder's has publications from around the world, spiced with small town journals. This long-time Minneapolis newsstand also carries videos. Shinder's has outlets in Minnetonka, downtown St. Paul and Edina.

Larkspur
122 North 4th Street
Minneapolis 55401
332-2140

Everybody who's anybody orders bouquets here! The originality of design and freshness of stock makes Larkspur a treasure trove for flower lovers. They provide each customer with a look that is new and lively. Owners Scott Rehovsky and Wendy Coggins know the floral trade and are creative geniuses!

International Market Square
275 Market Street
Minneapolis 55405
338-6250

The largest interior design center in the Midwest, this spectacular building houses over 200 showrooms. Every aspect of home and commercial decorating is represented. The most beautiful fabrics, materials, art pieces and design concepts from the world market are available. From the simple to the lavish, from stark to flamboyant, this wholesale market can produce astounding results.

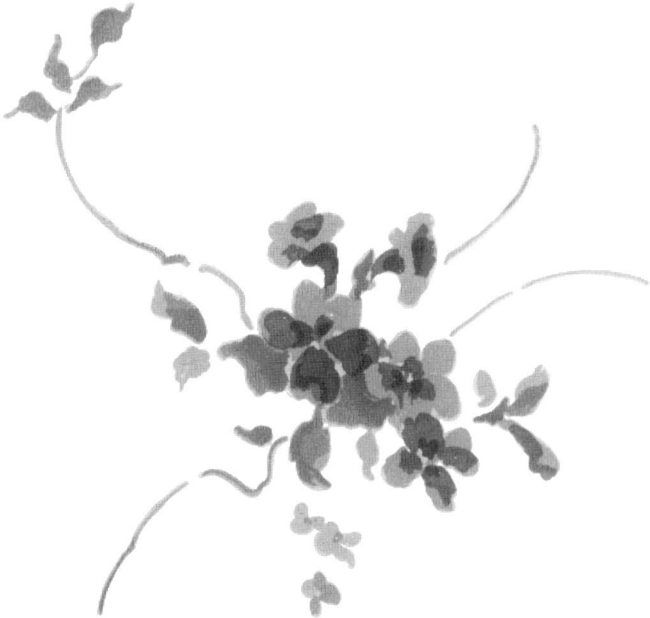

THE MINNEAPOLIS WAREHOUSE DISTRICT
Hennepin to 3rd Avenue, 2nd Street to 6th Street

Art galleries are the trademark of the Warehouse District. Small shops and studios come and go but are a recurring feature of this neighborhood that is also known for its trendy and upscale cuisine, its "Rebel Without a Cause" mood and a pace that is gentle by day and frenetic by night.

A stroll through the Warehouse District is a pilgrimage for the art lover. There is abundant architecture and spirited environment. Amid loading docks and industrial windows, retired smoke stacks and cobblestone streets, art abounds. Many styles and periods are offered, from local and regional works to pricey Picassos.

Restaurants are the district's true drawing card. Every taste can be satisfied with everything from a brief elixir or a complete dinner. These eateries include:

Acapulco -- Mexican foods and a DJ on weekends.
371-0828

Coyote -- American Southwestern cuisine.
338-1730

Gluek's Brewing Company -- Huge, hearty sandwiches in a great old building.
338-6621

Bocce -- A bar for basketball fans and hungry people.
332-1600

D'Amico Cucina -- Elegant and Italian and memorable.
338-2401

Jose's -- Mexican and American food and a patio on the alley.
333-5665

Loon Cafe -- Busy day and night with great food and active folks.
332-8342

Faegre's -- Good variety -- fresh fish, rack of lamb.
332-3515

Rosen's Bar & Grill -- Sports celebs, good food and good service.
338-1926

Pickled Parrot -- Southern & Southwestern foods & live musical performers.
332-0673

Chez Bananas -- Caribbean cuisine in the sun and fun.
340-0032

Urban Wildlife -- Basic bar foods for the fast crowd.
339-4665

New French Cafe -- Authentic French cuisine.
338-3790

Fine Line Music Cafe -- Lots of pasta plus rhythm & blues (cover charge).
338-8100

Cafe Brenda -- Tempting vegetarian fare.
342-9230

The Living Room -- International gourmet foods. Menu changes weekly.
343-0360

J. D. Hoyt's -- Hickory grilled steaks, salmon, catfish, chops.
301 Washington Avenue North
338-1560

Water's -- Sandwiches, soups and salads plus steak and chicken entrees.
333-1675

Runyon's -- Fresh soups, hot turkey sandwich and good looking people.
332-7158

Monte Carlo -- Meatloaf and egg salad sandwiches, salads, steaks.
333-5900

Nikki's -- Pastas, pizzas, tenderloins, blues and jazz.
340-9098

Origami -- A sushi bar with grilled fish, tempura, Kove steak.
333-8430

Cafe Solo -- Pizzas, pastas, sandwiches, huge fruit-flavored muffins.
332-7108

A map of galleries and restaurants is available at most establishments in the area.

RIVERPLACE and ST. ANTHONY MAIN

Riverplace and St. Anthony Main are located along the original Main Street in Minneapolis. The view of the Mississippi River and the downtown skyline makes Riverplace and St. Anthony Main an attractive spot for diners, shoppers and strollers.

DOWNTOWN ST. PAUL
Zip Code 55102

An ethnically rich, working class town, St. Paul's downtown offers a lot less stress and a bit more grace than its rival across the river.

The tone of downtown St. Paul is flavored by stately houses, well defined neighborhoods and cultural diversity. The curving streets and refurbished buildings among the new plazas and shopping centers give this city character and charm. Shopping centers in the downtown area include Galtier Plaza and St. Paul Center which was recently renamed The World Trade Center.

St. Paul is a curious blend of lace curtain manners and rambunctious progress. The shopper benefits from this mix. Headlined by Dayton's and Carson Pirie Scott, downtown St. Paul offers shoppers merchandise and services as diverse as its vital ethnicity.

Minnesota's only Four Star Hotel, the **Saint Paul Hotel** (292-9292) is a genuine highlight of downtown. This newly refurbished hostelry is the centerpiece of a neighborhood that includes the Ordway Music Theater, Landmark Center and Rice Park. The **St. Paul Grill** (22G-RILL) is a great spot to dine and to be seen. The Saint Paul Hotel is an important part of the downtown climate.

ST. PAUL LANDMARKS

Summit Avenue

The essence of old St. Paul is found along this spectacular thoroughfare. Lined with stately homes and architectural splendor, Summit has been called the country's best preserved Victorian boulevard. Once the home of James J. Hill and F. Scott Fitzgerald, Summit preserves the best traditions of the city's past. Foremost among the Summit Avenue mansions is the portentous Hill family home. It is as big and foreboding as its builder's presence in this city and state. Hill's art collection, pipe organ and massive library set a standard for extravagance. A walking tour of Summit on a summer evening will certainly take you back in time.

Winter Carnival

As much a St. Paul landmark as any building or bridge, the Winter Carnival is America's foremost winter celebration. The mythology of ice, snow and people tells the world that life is always to be celebrated. The highlight of the Winter Carnival is the ice palace which is a yearly tribute to stamina and the imagination.

DOWNTOWN ST. PAUL SHOPPING CENTERS

The World Trade Center

Truly the center of downtown St. Paul, the 36-story World Trade Center has over 110 specialty stores and restaurants, along with major department stores - Dayton's and Carson Pirie Scott.

Specialty stores present a wide variety of merchandise from the latest fashions to home accessories. Culinary choices range from elegant dining to a quick meal.

The World Trade Center has two courts for shopping and dining: Town Square and Town Court. Town Court has over 60 stores and restaurants including Carson Pirie Scott. Now called Cafesjian's Carousel and offering three minute rides, the refurbished Minnesota State Fair carousel has found a new home atop Town Square.

In the neighborhood . . .

Nakashian-O'Neil
23 West 6th Street
224-5465

There are those who say that Danny O'Neil is gilding the lily a bit too much, but life needs its excesses, and Nakashian-O'Neil serves it with expensive elan. The circular marble staircase, the furniture pieces, china, glassware and art represent the definitive le beau ideal in the Twin Cities. If the doorbell and by-appointment format do not discourage the faint-hearted, the prices will -- but go anyway! It's a collector's adrenaline surge!

Carriage Hill Plaza
350 St. Peter Street

Carriage Hill Plaza is reputed to have the best and safest parking ramp in downtown St. Paul.

Frank Murphy
Saint Peter at 5th
291-8844

The most venerable and distinguished women's clothier in the city, Frank Murphy transcends time and trend and remains the zenith of women's fashion. Frank Murphy is as closely linked to the culture of St. Paul as the State Capitol. They have complete ensembles that are the essence of fine taste. Their "giveaway" sales draw the masses to drastic markdowns.

Sonnie's
Coat Store and Main Store - 224-9400
Petite Store - 223-5424

One of four metro area stores, Sonnie's is simple, sophisticated elegance in women's clothing. They know the fashion market and are able to put together a smart look.

The two opticians at Carriage Hill Plaza are reputable and competitive. You will get quality eye care and a good look at **Northwest Opticians** (224-5621) and **Christy Optical** (222-4970). You can't go wrong at either place.

Walter Bradley Shoe Shine

The best shoe shine in St. Paul is done by Walter Bradley. He'll make you look like you stepped out of a band box. Treat yourself to the luxury.

John McLean Company
Galtier Plaza
175 East 5th Street
228-9746

Proper British tea is served in Minnesota through the innovations of John McLean and Company. Scones, shortbreads and the best of English teas are available to take home or enjoy at nearby tables. Bisto gravy mix, lemon and orange curds and Fortnum & Mason products make England seem like down the block.

Kramer Gallery
229 East 6th Street
228-1301

Specializing in American and European late 19th and 20th Century oil paintings, regional art and American Indian art and artifacts. Kramer also offers conservation, restoration and appraisal of fine art. This is an authoritative dealer.

GRAND AVENUE
Zip Code 55105

This is a thriving avenue of creative and ambitious entrepreneurs who have a sense of the marketplace and who know that their customers want the slightly unusual. We have selected from the many shops along the avenue those which are plainly grand.

The merchants of Grand Avenue have created a stratosphere of their own progressive design which has given them a prominent place on the local market. The once engaging pastime of strolling the avenue, browsing, buying, stopping to eat and chat is recreated on Grand. The concept has made this area an active, popular market. Four malls have aligned to offer a shopping experience not found elsewhere in the Twin Cities. The crowd here is a mix of the urban population, but certainly young couples, upscale moms and dads and striving singles abound.

VICTORIA CROSSING
Grand Avenue at Victoria

This is the crossroads of chic and value. Abundant, diverse, quality shops and services make Victoria Crossing a bright alternative to suburban malls. Merchandise here comes from around the world and is really not found in many other Twin City outlets. The intersection is made up of Victoria Crossing East, West and South. We'll tell you a bit about each.

VICTORIA CROSSING SOUTH
850 Grand Avenue

* * * * * * * * *

Ciatti's
292-9942

One of the most popular Italian spots in the metro area is Ciatti's. Their Northern and Southern Italian cuisine is always good, the service impeccable and the atmosphere -- bono! There are seven Ciatti's in the Twin Cities.

* * * * * * * * *

* * * * * * * * * *

Cafe Latte
224-5687

Its reputation is solid, its loyal customers are legion. There is no doubt that Cafe Latte is unparalleled in presenting desserts of splendid imagination and taste. Their light, unusual and healthy salads and sandwiches will alleviate the guilt of the epicurean tarts, pies, and pastries.

* * * * * * * * *

Just Grand
291-7434

If you can manage to try on clothes after a stop at neighboring Cafe Latte or Ciatti's, Just Grand has an outstanding selection of better ready-to-wear. They carry very chic sweaters and skirts.

VICTORIA CROSSING EAST
857 Grand Avenue

Old Mexico Shop, Inc.
293-3907

They venerate color and verve. The feeling here is of a bright and lovely culture where music, folk art, decor and lore tell the story of people. Their extensive collection of Mexican glassware, pottery, clothing and jewelry is presented joyfully. Unique items such as ceramic fishbowls with cats atop and wooden and papier-mache animals are the small pieces of life that the Old Mexico Shop offers.

Grand Spectacle
227-8198

Fashionable eyewear from Dior, Porsche and Ralph Lauren is complemented by affordable specs for the entire family. Their policy of meeting any verified price makes Grand Spectacle worth seeing.

Odegard Books
222-2711

Odegard took the first big step toward full-service book sales long ago and they have held their spot as the Twin Cities' favorite bookstore. There are titles to touch all tastes and temperaments in this cozy and usually crowded shop.

Paperworks
227-0890

The endless world of greeting cards is displayed here in cute, outrageous and tender variety. Wrap your sentiments in bold messages of caring with their gifts and papers.

VICTORIA CROSSING WEST
867 Grand Avenue

Periwinkle
221-0030

Like the periwinkle, a trailing plant of blues, whites and purples, this shop is a garden of texture, pattern and color. Slouchy velvet hats, flowered raincoats and umbrellas, needlepoint foot stools, boudoir pillows fill every niche at Periwinkle.

Annie's
228-9059

The clothes here are cool. They celebrate a fast and happy lifestyle. Annie's sales are worth waiting for.

Odegard Encore Books
222-2720

Just a hop, skip and a jump across the street from Odegard's in Victoria Crossing East, here you'll find discounted books of every description.

Minnesota Seasons
224-9349

There is a lot more than loons and lady slippers at this shop. Taste and see Minnesota's distinctive heritage. The year-round Christmas room features local artists. There is also a Minnesota Seasons at Bandana Square (647-0623).

Blue and White
291-2526

You heard it right. Everything is blue and white in this elegant and happy collection. There is Bev Doolittle art, cobalt glass by Blenko, vases, pictures, bowls, kaleidoscopes, baby gifts and frivolity!

MILTON MALL
917 Grand Avenue

* * * * * * * * *

Leeann Chin
291-0545

Leeann Chin is serving the metro area her own brand of Chinese cuisine in astonishing volume and variety. You may dine in, carry out or have dinner brought to your door. Leeann Chin has become a household name in the Cities. There are 13 Leeann Chin delis and three restaurants in the Twin Cities.

* * * * * * * * *

Salisbury Flower Market
291-7212

A European style flower shop whose stock includes over 100 varieties of imported and domestic flowers, Salisbury is the floral alternative. Their inventory of the exotic and exquisite can bring shoppers to a new appreciation of the world of plants and flowers. Salisbury carries dried stems and wreaths and will custom make dried arrangements. Also at Calhoun Square (825-1991).

In Vision
291-0318

If you want glasses that are tailored to your look and lifestyle, stop by In Vision. Spend some time sorting through the almost overwhelming display of styles, colors, designs and attitudes. Cast off that nerdish image and let the world see you in glasses from this high style optical boutique. There are six In Vision outlets in the Twin Cities.

Breedlove's
222-8745

Very sophisticated clothing for women is de rigueur at Breedlove's. Great jewelry, hats, accessories will make customers look like a million bucks.

Little Dickens
293-0444

They will costume yours in adorable clothing that will knock the dickens right out of the most trying child. Their guideline is impeccable, 100% cotton fashions that will give your children that picture perfect look. If your precious ones are infants through age 7 for boys or infants through size 14 for girls, Little Dickens has something you'll want.

Depth of Field
222-5356

Your home can become as cushy and colorful as the atmosphere at Depth of Field. Their expert consultation on fabrics, colors and motifs helps customers make sound decisions. There is a great world of comfort and style here. Also in Minneapolis (339-6061).

---

* * * * * * * * *

Benjamin's Restaurant

Popular, comfortable, good tasting , Benjamin's is a restaurant for the family. The home cooking and wide variety of staples make this a welcome respite from the woes of shopping.

* * * * * * * * *

Out on the street again . . .

Cooks of Crocus Hill
877 Grand Avenue
228-1333

Picture-perfect kitchen accessories. Not only will your kitchen look great, it will have the technology to maximize your culinary skills. Exquisite ceramic serving dishes, gourmet foods and Alice Factor baguettes make Cooks of Crocus Hill a fine shop.

Broomhouse Street
889 Grand Avenue
224-3367

If home could be like this! A darling shop bursts with comfort and conviviality. Have coffee or tea while you peruse antiques and reproductions, handmade jewelry -- and to replace that passe kitchen witch, they have guardian kittens, cows and bunny angels.

The Red Balloon Bookshop
891 Grand Avenue
224-8320

You can spot this store by the tree trunk sculpture of "The Three Bears" at curbside. The victim of Dutch Elm disease, the 11 foot trunk was converted to a work of art by Dennis Roghair. The Red Balloon has captured the magic appeal of childhood and presents it in books (non-fiction and foreign language included), toys, videos, and posters. They know the wonder and whimsy that is part of being a kid.

The Bibelot Shop
1082 Grand Avenue
222-0321

The French call it small and precious. We call Bibelot a new look. They can fill the secret corners of your life with goods ranging from address and guest books to kitchenware and jewelry, from clothes and cards to tie dye and books on how to live. Also on Como Avenue (646-5651).

Creative Kidstuff
1085 Grand Avenue
222-2472

Find out why this store, packed with innovative toys, music, art and craft projects and games has been named "Best Toy Store" many times. A knowledgeable staff will advise you on wonderfully creative stuff to stimulate kids *and* adults. *Low ceilings: Mind your head if you're tall! Also Linden Hills (927-0653) and Minnetonka (540-0022).

Needlepoint Allie
1110 Grand Avenue
228-0981

Create your piece of history. With the help of this complete needlepoint shop, you can make the creations that your guests will admire and your grandchildren will treasure. They specialize in custom design. Classes in needlepoint are offered.

Maggie's Corner
1128 Grand Avenue
298-0913

This house is jam packed with large and small pieces of the past. A treasure can be found here. The hunt is worth it. Maggie does estate sales, appraisals and consignment.

Cottageware Homestore
1129 Grand Avenue
224-2933

This is a complete home furnishing store with a European appeal, objects old and new and decorating ideas for the person who likes the unusual.

Baby Grand
1137 Grand Avenue
224-4414

Your child deserves the best and you're likely to find it at Baby Grand. Outfits for infants to size 4-toddler that will transform even the terrible two's into little darlings. They carry cribs, car seats, bedding and all the amenities of babyhood.

Celebration Designs
1457 Grand Avenue
690-4344

Artists and crafters give homage to the spiritual in their paintings, sculpture, graphics, wooden carvings, ceramics and creches. This gallery of sacred arts and crafts, owned by five women, celebrates life.

Hungry Mind Book Store
1648 Grand Avenue
699-0587

This store is a gathering place for area readers and writers. Readings by the likes of Garrison Keillor and Tobias Wolf are part of the Hungry Mind's appeal. The personnel know literature and thrive on living their work. Along with fascinating and diverse titles, the Hungry Mind supplies an intellectual home for the community. The Table of Contents restaurant is adjacent and enjoyable (699-6595).

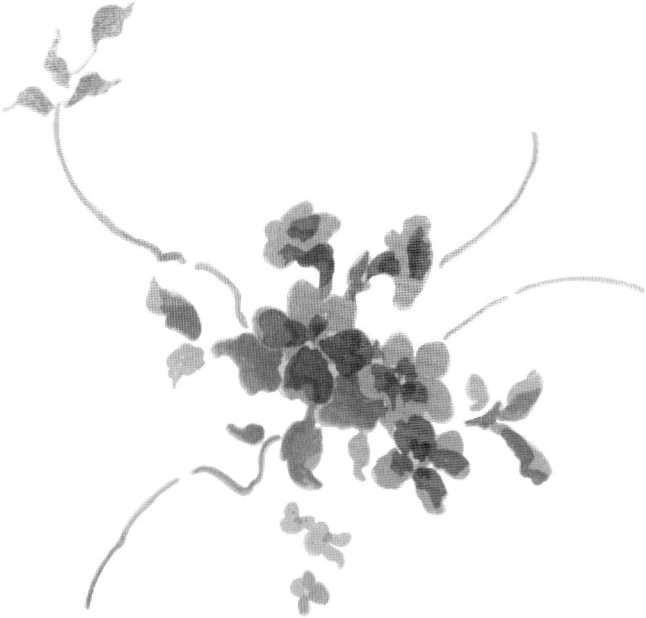

UPTOWN MINNEAPOLIS
Zip Code 55408

Uptown is where prep, funk and yuppie meet under the glow of a constantly lit urban candle. It boasts over 75 shops courting new merchandise in old buildings. Here Bohemian tastes and a sense of adventure result in a unique mixture of tastes. Uptown has a young, frenetic spirit that is a microcosm of the metro area. It casts a spell on shoppers and moves them quickly through a colorful queue of shops, restaurants and concessions. Door by door, shop after shop, Uptown is a fast and serious mover in the stream of urban life. Anchored by Calhoun Square, a three-level indoor mall with a distinct Soho flavor, Uptown is the fastest growing marketplace in Minneapolis-St. Paul. The Square is open every day, but individual shop and restaurant hours vary. Services include a post office, medical and dental clinics and shoe repair. Figlio, one of several restaurants in the Square, was selected by <u>Metropolitan Home</u> magazine as "One of the 10 Best Bistros in America." The shops include clothing stores for men, women and children whose tastes tend toward the avant-garde. A bookstore, candy, cookie and natural food shops and some of the best toy and kitchenware inventories in the cities are all found in this busy people-filled center.

Uptown is the site of summer festivities including a June jazz festival, Aquatennial events in July and the massive Uptown Art Fair in August. There is food for all tastes and budgets, from the tasteful Lucia's to the great breads, soups and omelets on the menu at Pam Sherman's Bakery. There are delis, yogurt and ice cream shops, plentiful croissants and sufficient pubs.

elements
2941 Hennepin
824-5300

Glass, chrome, leather, lucite and plastics are found throughout. Framed art works by Kadinsky and McKnight and Italian leather sofas offer a starkly modern look. Stemware, mugs, glass accessories in a variety of styles and patterns are designed to dress up your home and give some pizazz to your lifestyle. Also at Roseville (633-3515) and Southdale (866-0631).

A Fine Romance
2912 Hennepin Avenue South
822-4144

This shop is the leader of the Uptown pack. Hand-made journals, antique items, very unique jewelry, imported soaps and gifts, imported cards, gift wrap and enclosures -- paper products extraordinaire -- are among the exquisite items at A Fine Romance. They make the avant-garde seem cozy.

Shoe Zoo
3146 Hennepin Avenue
823-3988

As lively and expressive as childhood, the Shoe Zoo handles domestic and imported children's shoes. Your kids will be high stepping in high fashion.

Gabriela's
1404 West Lake
822-1512

The motion pictures of the 40's and 50's with Bogart and Bacall, Bette Davis and Joan Crawford were known for stylish costumes. Those wardrobes can be yours in this fabulous collection of vintage clothing and costume jewelry. Dresses, suits, sweaters and pants and everything to accessorize fills this shrine to past styles.

CALHOUN SQUARE
3001 Hennepin Avenue

Benetton
822-6696

Benetton jazzes up classic style and color and brings it smack-dab into today's changing clothing market. Whether you set or follow the trends, you'll outfit with splash and sophistication at Benetton. There are seven Benetton stores in the Twin Cities including a children's store at the Galleria and an outlet store in St. Paul.

Bay Street Shoes
824-5574

This is a blockbuster store and one of the few that carries shoes for women and men. Since 1984 Bay Street has presented strong fashion footwear in a mixture of comfort, lifestyle, career and dress shoes. Their lines include Nine West, Easy Spirit, Vittorio Ricci, Rockport, Jazz, Dexter for women. Men look great in Zodiac, Cole-Haan, Johnston & Murphy, Dexter, Timberland, Rockport, Kenneth Cole. The harness boot by Code West for women and the Nature Shoe by Glen for men help define this store's powerful style. Year after year, Bay Street has been rated best shoe store by the Twin Cities Reader and City Pages. Their imaginative inventory is supported by top notch customer service. A gem of a store.

Kitchen Window
824-4417

This place is a joy for professional and amateur chefs. They carry a large collection at the best prices of Calphalon, Chantal and All-Clad. Kitchen Window also boasts the largest pot rack selection in the Upper Midwest. Hard-to-find kitchen gadgets, bakeware, French porcelains and glassware are also available.

Borders Book Shop
825-0336

Borders is a panoply of literary fare touching every curiosity and conscience. They have it all here, organized for convenience and ease of selection.

Schlampp's
3001 Hennepin Avenue
823-7272

Schlampp's has been dressing Minneapolis women since 1919. Their selection of upper end dresses ($400 to $600) include Jean Marc and Morton Miles. They can accessorize any ensemble with handbags, hats and jewelry. Schlampp's has a spectacular fur salon. They carry Alexandra de Markoff beauty supplies and are the exclusive handler in the Twin Cities of the magnificent French perfume Secret of Venus.

doo dah!
822-7244

A tableau of merriment, doo dah! will spruce up your life with its imaginative selection of cards, unique gifts (the mummy tins are a must) and decorator items. They handle a gamut of greeting cards from cutsie to risque. Cutouts of George and Barbara Bush and social and political statement T-shirts are but a few wonders in this vast collection. Quite a "with it" shop.

Toy Boat
822-5066

This isn't just for kids. Toy Boat has a complete line of high quality, unusual toys in the moderate to high price range. Brand names include Darda, Lego, Gund, Steiff and Dover. There are also hand made dolls, dollhouses and furnishings. Grand Avenue (293-0313) and Galleria (920-9221) as well.

Roomers Gallery
822-9490

Unique, original works from various media are presented at Roomers Gallery. Handmade paper, sculptured ceramics, hand painted picture frames are among what owner Julie Landa calls "serious whimsy." They handle local and regional artists but also enter the national market to locate a collection to which most folks do not have access. If you are serious about art or if you just love life, Roomers Gallery will appeal to you.

Body Language
822-4590

Your body speaks to you and it frequently says "I want to look great." The response you need to give is found at Body Language. They have everything for the active, exercising woman. Even if you aren't too serious about the fitness fad, you can play the part swimmingly with tights and leotards of every description, headbands, socks, swimsuits, jumpsuits, sweats and cover-ups that are action oriented. Tennis anyone?

Textilis
822-3198

A premier house of fabrics with lush, flashy, intricate, delicate, bold designs. Over 200 fabrics to choose from in varied content and theme. They offer free in-home consultation on custom made draperies, blinds, slipcovers, bedding, table and bath linens. This is the best quality and a high fashion look.

C. P. More
824-4333

The walls and shelves are full of "Lunch at the Ritz" earrings and other jewelry, upbeat hats, handbags, belts and scarves. C. P. More buys the latest and the unique.

Bacio
824-5352

A collection of funky and slightly out-of-the-mainstream clothing from New York and Los Angeles design firms. The Basco shirts for men are lined, hand-stitched and gorgeous. European industrial patterned shirts by Armand Basi, Kikit sweaters, Naturalife for women and rayon shirts by Cape are among other featured lines.

Dimitrius
822-3166

Black is the best seller in this shop that specializes in the European casual look. Knit jackets and sweaters in earth tones, dramatic ties and business suits are offered in a slick setting.

Hollywood High
824-2762

The trendy goods are geared for the young-at-heart and the high tech shopper. Included are party clothes, African jewelry, wild earrings and lots of studs and rhinestones. The visit can be remembered with a photo booth shot for one dollar.

Latitudes Map and Travel Store
823-3742

Everything for actual and armchair travelers, from maps and globes, atlases and travel guides to durable luggage and travel accessories. Presentations by travelers and authors are frequently scheduled.

Tom Schmidt Salon
827-5595

The "Star Search" set could get their start at Tom Schmidt. This is a totally modern concept dressed in slick, provocative decor which says that the beauty business is serious stuff. They offer complete hair and body treatment for men and women.

Leaving Calhoun Square . . .

Ragstock
1433 Lake Street
823-6690

Looking somewhat like the greatest rummage sale in the world, Ragstock outfits the brave and the offbeat in vintage suits and dresses, Hawaiian shirts, military garb, Italian pajamas and silk bathrobes. They also have new clothing including a great selection of spandex and cottons and casuals. The prices are low and there is always a wide and changing selection. Also at Dinkytown (331-6064) and 7th Street Warehouse (333-8520).

---

intoto
3105 Hennepin Avenue
822-2414

A class operation! You're always greeted with a welcoming offer of bottled spring water as you enter intoto, where both American and European designers are featured. They are the exclusive Twin Cities outlet for Think Tank (for both men and women). Men's designers also include New Republic, Wilkie-Rodriquz, Jekyll and Hyde of London. For women the wonderful Bettina Budewig and Isda. A selection of ties includes Carrot and Gibbs bows. A unique item at intoto is the collection of restored vintage fountain pens.

For a quiet respite, just six blocks south of this hectic corner is a showplace for some of the finest examples of Tiffany glass in the world -- the unique windows in the Lakewood Cemetery Chapel. Also located in the cemetery is the grave site of Vice President Hubert H. Humphrey.

The cemetery and the chapel are open to the public during daylight hours.

EDINA

Edina was built by the pre-yuppie generation. It has been said that you cannot move to Edina; you must achieve Edina. Achievement is the winning ticket, whether it be in its schools, its neighborhoods or its retail market. Edina comes by its reputation naturally and spectacularly.

This southwest suburb of Minneapolis is a consumer heaven. The home of successful entrepreneurs and professionals, its shopping centers thrive on consumers who also know style and value. Edina is the home of the first enclosed mall in the world, Southdale, built by the Dayton family in 1956. It was expanded in 1990 and remains the most profitable and distinguished retail center in the Twin Cities.

Shopping in Edina begins at 44th Street and France Avenue, where the village of Morningside once straddled the cities of Minneapolis and Edina. Now officially Edina, the neighborhood retains its independent character and its "Father Knows Best" style.

Some of the best bargains in Edina are found at garage and estate sales where household goods from the areas most prestigious suburb become available to the intrepid and patient. Edinians are known as the ultimate consumers so even their second-hand has utility and class.

Nearby on France Avenue is:

Durr Ltd.
4386 France Avenue
Edina 55410
925-9146

In an historic old building in a quiet Edina neighborhood, Donna Durr has created a home furnishings store with room after room of lovely settings filled with fine antiques and reproductions. In 1984 when Donna couldn't find the furnishings she wanted to display in her builder husband's European-styled spec houses, she purchased country antiques from England and ultimately opened her own shop. Now Donna and her knowledgeable design staff advise customers on every aspect of interior design from furniture to fabrics, antiques to dried botanicals. Durr Ltd. has a gift registry for busy customers and a newsletter to inform and inspire customers with interior design news and special events at Durr Ltd.

50th & FRANCE
Zip Code 55424

The corner of 50th and France is the "downtown" of this century-old suburb. This is home to more than 100 retail shops. There is also a Lund's supermarket catering to the fussiest palates in the area and Clancy's Drug with delivery service and an old-fashioned soda fountain.

R S V P
922-7777

A stationery specialty store whose merchandise ranges in style and price, RSVP is known for the quality of its inventory as well as its service. When looking for personalized letter papers, wedding and party announcements, birth announcements, holiday cards or greeting cards, RSVP will guide you in your selections.

Burwick 'N Tweed
926-9551

This men's clothier carries very good labels including Joseph Abboud, Zanella, Falke sportswear and suits from Germany, Haupt, Robert Comstock, Winston Woods and Nanibon sweaters from Italy. They combine the best looks from American and European designers to give an updated traditional look. Burwick provides tailoring and custom shirt service.

Belleson's
3908 West 50th Street
927-4694

Belleson's is a neighborhood store that carries men's and women's clothing with international labels. In operation since 1948, Belleson's has become known for quality clothing that lasts through the years. They have one of the best shoe departments in the area and their in-house alterations and tailoring shop is an expert operation.

J-Michael Galleries
3916 West 50th Street
920-6070

This fine art shop specializes in watercolors by local and regional artists. They also have limited editions, some sculptures and some wildlife paintings. J-Michael has excellent representations of the genres.

Chico's
4954 France Avenue South
925-5474

Chico's believes that fashion can be comfortable. Their garment-died clothing has European styling and can be mixed and matched. Sweaters, sweatshirts, shorts and cruisewear are available year-round. Owner Dana Atherton can dress people from head to toe with her excellent wardrobing service. Also at Eden Prairie Center (943-1909) and Wayzata (476-1812).

Wild Child
4948 France Avenue South
926-5675

This is what kids are supposed to look like. In natural fibers and wonderful colors, infants and children can look casually elegant. Color coordinated, died to match outfits which can be used in so many ways and for so many occasions make dressing your child quite a bit of fun.

White Oak Gallery
3939 West 50th Street
922-3575

The watercolors of Barbara Hultmann are available only at White Oak Gallery. Her florals are unmatched in color and depth. There is mixed media here in both traditional and representational pieces. The works of Ellen Diederich, Indian pieces, glassware. They also do custom framing.

Simply Splendid
3939 West 50th Street
922-6830

This modern mercantile has an eclectic collection of gifts. Items for the baby, cards, jewelry, kids clothing, art and decorative pieces, fresh coffee and coffee beans. They let the imagination run wild and have come up with some splendid goods.

Rainbow Fine Art Gallery
3929 West 50th Street
922-5920

Quite good art from the East and West coasts as well as Brazil and this region are at this impressive gallery. A local artist featured is Alexandra Jacobs, wife of high-profile financier Irwin Jacobs.

The Cottage Sampler
3915 West 50th Street
925-9672

Gift items and home accessories are displayed in this country atmosphere. Salt-glazed pottery, linens, afghans, dried flower arrangements. Merchandise at The Cottage Sampler is not from large manufacturers so much of it is few-of-a-kind items or pieces that are not available other places.

Tidepool Gallery
3909 West 50th Street
926-1351

"By the sea, by the sea, by the beautiful sea." Ah yes, everything that is fresh and romantic about the sea is captured in this gift and decorator shop. Seashells and coral are used in every manner of gifts. Framed shells, lovely pill boxes are here in a wonderfully imaginative collection.

Periwinkles
5004 France Avenue South
925-4221

Make every occasion an event! Periwinkles has scoured the landscape and come up with a spectacular collection of greeting cards, gift wrap, note paper, small gifts and balloons. They will fit your fancy and make the recipients of your correspondence or generosity wondering how you do it.

McMuffee's Ltd.
5014 France Avenue South
926-2889

McMuffee's makes an endless pursuit of accumulating a unique and extensive collection of women's fashions. From cottage industries, to custom made, to imported, they offer easy-to-wear clothing in colorful and robust styles. Dress lines include Maggie Breen, Kathryn Conover and Sara Campbell. Sportswear by Segrets and Kenneth Gordon. McMuffee's has an international teddy bear sweater, $500 Berek handknits, block and motif sweaters and sweaters of every style and price. McMuffee's appreciates the unique feelings that only sweaters can convey.

The Club Room
5016 France Avenue South
920-3684

This could well be the scene of a knitting bee or a quilting. The cozy atmosphere brings fanciers of needlework who want high quality yarns, threads, floss and supplies. An extensive inventory of patterns will impress even the most experienced crafter.

Accessory Collection
5018 France Avenue South
922-0111

Do you wonder where decorator magazines get the accent pieces that make rooms look so opulent and rich? Stop here for a glimpse of the distinctive and unusual ornaments and finery that will fill the corners of your home with high style and great form. Art work, vases and jardinieres, lamps, linens, pillows and figurines from around the world are shown in this extensive and varied collection. Decorate your life with the best of taste. This darling shop with a greenhouse front is tucked behind the Edina Theater and behind McMuffee's -- don't miss it!

Grethan House
5041 France Avenue South
926-8725

This is not the department store look, but an individualized approach that provides each customer with their own fashion statement. A visit to this shop is like entering someone's home where you are a guest of honor. Grethan House is for women who want to develop their own look. They are thoroughly experienced in all aspects of fashion and carry Barry Brickin and Harriet Selwin dresses, shoes by Robert Clergerie and Andrea Carras.

N etc. is located in the same space and provides the finishing touches. Hats, hose, scarves, purses selected with individual flair in mind.

Shelly's Tall Fashions
5029 France Avenue South
920-2668

Shopping can be frustrating for the tall woman. Too often pants and skirts are just too short. Shelly's carries excellent brands including Pendleton, London Fog, Harve Bernard, Eve Laurel and Kensington Square. The staff at Shelly's knows the needs of their special customers and assists them in finding separates, dresses, pants, coats, blouses and skirts that will enhance their appearance.

Wuollet Bakery
3608 West 50th Street
922-4341

Step inside a Wuollet Bakery and your life will never be the same. The gleaming showcases, the aroma of fresh-baked confections and the array of picture-perfect breads, cookies, muffins and cakes transports customers to a new experience. Wuollet is known all over the Twin Cities for memorable desserts. The tortes, including torte diplomatico, chocolate porcelain or marzipan torte, are sumptuous and romantic. The breads, with their European texture, are simply the best. An added attraction is that customers may sample the ware. Also at St. Paul (292-9035) and Wayzata (473-8621).

Banners To Go
5029 France Avenue South
925-2883

If you need to get the point across in a very big way, this store will design a sign or banner to suit your need. They have paper, laminated and vinyl banners, magnetic signs, show cards, silk screened signs and sign holders. Present your logo or crest in living color from the many styles and types at Banners To Go.

The Children's General Store
3933 West 50th Street
925-2841

A happy place to shop for infant through preteen girls and infant to prep boys. They carry unique clothing, special hand-made items, pins, earrings and accessories (hair bows, socks) and all the latest fashion for the young set. A great spot to find that perfect birthday gift. It's wild and fun.

Shoe Allee
3940 West 50th Street
926-9922

A jazzy and colorful array of medium-priced shoes for day and evening, plus handbags, shoe clips and costume jewelry may be found here. Wonderful sales.

SOUTHDALE

On France Avenue at 66th Street is Southdale, the dean of American retail malls. The new skylighted Dayton's store has been called "the temple of commerce" with Fresco paintings, statuary and objet d'art.

Southdale Center also includes J.C. Penney, Carson Pirie Scott, apparel and accessory shops, electronic shops, food shops and restaurants, card and gift shops, hobby and leisure activity stores, shops that specialize in home furnishings, jewelry stores, and a drug store. There are also optical, hairstyling, financial, postal and airline services. The Children's Barber (922-3343) in the lower level is designed to make hair cutting a breeze for kids and mom and dad. The Southdale courtyard is the site of concerts, exhibitions and community events. A spectacular addition of 35 new stores in 1991 adds to Southdale's already glittering crown.

THE GALLERIA
3510 West 70th Street
Zip Code 55435

Just a block from Southdale on France Avenue is the Galleria -- a blatantly and beautifully upscale shopping center. The Galleria boasts 35 absolutely lavish stores filled with everything you don't need, but can't resist. There is valet parking on weekends.

Stores in the Galleria and appearing elsewhere in this book:

>Barrie Pace, Ltd. (927-4558)
>Benetton (920-7204)
>In Vision (920-5458
>Laura Ashley (920-2811)
>Liemandt's (927-4558)
>Pottery Barn (925-0224)
>Sonnie's (929-3022)
>Toy Boat (920-9221)
>Urban Traveler (922-3672)
>Water Street Clothing (927-6336)
>Williams-Sonoma (925-0039)

Galleria restaurants and delis include:

>Ciatti's (920-3338)
>Ediner (925-4008)
>Good Earth (925-1001)
>Rosebud Grocery (926-1623)
>Vie de France (929-9363)

Cedric's
925-3424

Cedric and Norma Kirchner run Minnesota's most prominent family-owned high fashion store. The women's clothing choices range from wild, multi-colored sweaters by Escada at $1,200 to wear-forever classic sweaters at $150. There are frequent trunk shows. Featured designers include Louis Feraud, St. John Knits, Crisca and Ungaro. They have a Gottex Swim Shop, a wonderful fur salon and appropriate accessories for all outfits. A welcome recent addition is fashion director Edward Holmberg, talented long-time apparel expert and commentator. Adjacent to the women's store is Cedric's for Men, claiming to "make a suit to fit anyone." They carry Canali, Lubian, Prandina, Brioni, Zanella and Mondo and feature Countess Mara ties and Bally Shoes.

Liemandt's
927-4558

Liemandt's avoids trends and offbeat fashions. The right label and the right look are important here. Dobbs, Hart, Schaffner & Marx, Austin Reed, Burberry's, Gant hold their place in the often skittish clothing market. Under the direction of founder Jack Liemandt, this company has maintained a high standard of men's and women's dress. They appeal to professional people who put stock in how they look. Stores also at City Center (332-8473), Ridgedale (546-0700), St. Paul (222-8431), Burnsville (435-8668) and Rosedale (636-1744). Barrie Pace Ltd. also has stores at the Galleria (927-4558) and Gaviidae Common (338-8288).

Joseph of Chicago
929-6430

The best shoes and handbags in the Twin Cities are found here. Jose knows more about shoes than the little old woman. Their lines include Andrea Pfister, Escada, Walter Steiger, Anne Klein, Stuart Weitzman, Ferragamo, Cole-Haan and YSL. Judith Leiber handbags are featured. Jewelry lines are from artists throughout the world including sterling by Brent Schoenfeld and brass and semi-precious stones from Jose Perez of Argentina. The prices are high, but you are rewarded with gift certificates and sale notices if you join their Frequent Buyer Program.

Nancy Lawrence fine apparel sizes 14-26
925-9305

For the discriminating woman, a shop that doesn't discriminate. Nancy Lawrence chooses up-to-the-minute styles and colors in women's sizes 14 to 26. With their casual wear and special occasion dresses, large jewelry and eye for proper tailoring, no one need take second best in fashion. Understanding and helpful sales assistants will model their merchandise.

D. W. Stewart's
920-5757

Big and tall men can step out with the best of them with a wardrobe from D.W. Stewart's. Intended for men six feet and taller, Stewart's has suits, shoes, casual and sportswear from such prominent designers as Perry Ellis and Chaps by Ralph Lauren. It's a great big world and everyone can have a piece of the fashion action.

Truffles Chocolatier
920-0828

America's insatiable passion for chocolate reaches a new height at Truffles Chocolatier. This is a festival of sublime tastes from gourmet popcorn and low-calorie yogurt to Mint Lentils and Swedish Peps. There is delight in all price ranges and the packaging is a gift in itself. Bright yellow boxes are the proper cheery presentation for this fabulous chocolate.

Shari Rose, Ltd.
928-0020

Shari Rose has home accessories and gifts with the flavor of the English and French countryside. They carry Holden china group and charming, handmade wedding accessories including ring bearer pillows, frames, photo albums, guest books and pens. Their headline item is fine art. Marty Bell lithographs are foremost in this interesting collection.

Mondi
925-0788

At Mondi you will find superb women's fashions in the medium to high-price range. You will also find styles that are bold and distinctive. Owners Judy and Tom Reichert manage a store that is aggressive in its presentation of very good merchandise from the German-owned company that gives the store its name. Each season Mondi has nine to twelve collections. Everything from shoes to accessories to complete an ensemble. Within a collection there may be as many as a dozen tops including sweaters, jackets and blouses to go with any bottom. The total look!

MainStreet Kids
929-1446

Touting children's clothing in updated traditional styles, MainStreet Kids is one of the best kid's clothing stores in the Twin Cities. Owner Stacey Bame has an eye for this market and a zest for her work that provides not only top quality but great customer service. She is not interested only in sales volume, but also in providing clothes that younger family members can wear someday. The lines are very good, Polo Ralph Lauren, Gant, Adrienne Vittadini, Florence Eiseman and Sylvia Whyte.

Main Street Outfitters
920-4323

As the name implies, the goods here are for just any ole' body who wants a look that is comfortable and colorful. Theme sweaters and tops by Cambridge Dry Goods and buffalo flannel skirts along with shirts, jeans, cords, coats, hats, scarves
and gloves offer both casualness and tradition to the variety of shoppers who keep coming back to Main Street.

Maternal Instincts
927-4527

Their well-tailored clothing for the mother-to-be allows life to go on in a normal, happy way while waiting for that special arrival. There is lingerie and swimwear and generally upscale clothing. Maternal Instincts has stores at Calhoun Square (824-8100) and in St. Paul (690-1969).

The Real Nancy Drew
926-1977

The newest angle from Nancy Drew, the zany artist from Niles, Michigan, offers gifts and decorative items that are not found elsewhere, except perhaps in fancy. Art work, hand painted furniture (rocking chairs, tables, birch stools, dressers), free-spirited clothing, personal and domestic accessories are presented in daring and colorful concepts and haphazard motifs. They say, "This is not a normal store." They are right.

Frost & Budd
922-6058

Masters of the town and country look, Frost & Budd offers china, glassware, gifts and accessories in wide variety with sophisticated styling. There is a large outdoor/garden department offering bird houses and feeders, garden sculptures and statuary, weather vanes, sundials, mailboxes, doormats, barbecue tools, croquet and horseshoes. Their goods are very handsome. With designs that portray the golfer, hunter, sailor or polo player, Frost & Budd can dress up an interior, provide a gift, augment a hobby or present a lovely table setting. A wide range of unusual and unique gourmet food items is also offered. Also in Wayzata (473-1442).

Jonci Petites
926-7061

Half of the women in America are under 5 feet 4 inches in height. It is to this population that Jonci Petites brings a complete line of women's wear. Dresses, suits, sportswear, special occasion frocks, winter coats and raincoats, sleepwear, lingerie and leather pieces make Jonci truly the specialist for small women who want to look great. Labels such as Anne Klein, Ellen Tracy and Liz Claiborne are foremost among the excellent lines carried here.

Shades of Vail
920-0857

Shades of Vail has sunglasses to satisfy every taste and pocketbook. Sunglasses make a statement about the wearer and here you will find some trait of your personality about which you want to tell the world. From France, there is Christian Dior and Vuarnet. There are ski glasses, beach glasses, sports glasses and aviator glasses. If you have prescription lenses, save the day with a pair of wraparounds.

Three Rooms Up
926-1774

If you have an appreciation for quality and the unusual this is a 20-year-old jewel. Nothing commercial graces the shelves. The ceramics, glass, sculpture, turned wood, jewelry, paintings and prints are original hand works of nearly 100 artists and craftspeople from across the country, all presented in a light and contemporary setting.

Kafte
926-8655

At Kafte they realize that coffee is truly the international drink and they provide it with unrivaled flavor and style. Unique among coffee retailers, Kafte roasts their own beans and brews four fresh flavors each day. All the tools and equipment that have become part of the American consumer's fascination with coffee, from espresso machines to tea eggs, are part of their always new and expanding inventory. Also at Calhoun Square (824-1368) and downtown (339-3838).

Gabberts Furniture & Design
927-1500

Gabberts is the premier dealer of home furnishings in the Twin Cities. The newly re-designed and redecorated store carries their complete range of furniture styles, from traditional to contemporary. Gabberts Artifacts, Design Studio, Fine Arts and Furniture Galleries comprise the largest store in The Galleria. Their Odd's 'n Ends room offers some of the best buys in town. Free interior design seminars are frequently offered. Complimentary coffee, hot chocolate and cookies are available downstairs and the television is always on to occupy the children while parents shop.

len druskin
927-7923

Len Druskin has been in the women's clothing market for years and has a hunter's eye for fashion. The concept at len druskin is to mix seemingly discordant styles and fabrics to create a new and daring look. The concept works. Tons of Helen Hsu separates, Gispa knits and Misha Moon silk and woven pieces are brought together in glorious texture and color. There are fancy clothes with sequins, rhinestones and lame and a wide variety of well selected casual and dress wear.

epitome
920-2978

There is more than clothing at epitome. Three foot licorice sticks and entertaining little millet dolls, picture frames and personalized stationery add to the attractions. But sophisticated clothing by Joan Vass, DKNY, Ralph Lauren, Vittadini, Bettina Reidel and Calvin Klein Sport are the mainstay of this store that always has new ways to dress up the lives of its customers.

Pappagallo
925-3388

They can deck you out from head to toe at this innovative shoe and accessory shop. High heel pumps covered with sequins and ballet-style metallic flats are found among hand-painted sweatshirts, wild and racy jewelry, turtlenecks and T-shirts in interesting and crazy patterns and all kinds of accessories.

Barnes & Noble
920-0633

A booklover's extravaganza, Barnes & Noble bookstores purvey the intellectual and literary stock of America and the world. The technological revolution notwithstanding, Barnes & Noble proves that America is still reading. Their super stores stock more than 100,000 titles and more than 200,000 volumes in 16,000 square feet. Each store also carries more than 1,200 newspapers and magazines from around the world. Barnes & Noble originated the everyday discount concept, offering bargain books at 20-80% off the publisher's list price, and everyday discounts on "New York Times Bestsellers." Also at Roseville (631-1125), Ridgehaven (541-0508) and Burnsville (898-4505).

Schmitt Music Company
920-5080

Their 125-seat recital hall is available to the public at no charge and their 31 lesson studios are part of the comprehensive merchandising effort at Schmitt Music. Since 1896 this company has been providing instruments, lessons and accessories to Minneapolis musicians. From sheet music to grand pianos to guitar picks, Schmitt keeps the music playing in the Twin Cities. At eight locations, Schmitt is the area's foremost professional music specialist.

Rocco Altobelli
920-5006

The name is synonymous with style and innovation in the hair industry. Rocco Altobelli at the Galleria is the largest hair salon in the Twin Cities with 50 stations and a full-service spa. The spa offers body wraps, facials and massages. Founder Rocco Altobelli has gained international attention for breaking ground in the industry and developing the most advanced techniques anywhere. The result of these efforts is a large clientele who sport the best look in the Twin Cities.

Muggins Doll House, Inc.
922-8044

Muggins Doll House builds memories for children and has a treasury of dolls and animals that customers can cherish. Their doll houses have all the imaginative details from mom and dad to pies in the oven. The miniatures, stuffed animals, dolls, games, books and toys are not meant to be casual or passing purchases. They are the stuff which enriches childhood and provides experiences that will last forever.

My Oh My
927-0267

Patterned boxes which house your goodies and decorate your room, greeting cards that say what most people can't, perfume bottles that will enchant the receiver and thrill the collector, sachets that can fill a drawer or a room with fragrance and stationery that is unique and personal are at My oh My here and at their sister store Doo Dah in Calhoun (822-7244).

A Pea In The Pod
925-9770

Expectant mothers can look fashionable and feel comfortable in maternity clothes from A Pea In The Pod. Made of natural fabrics and featuring styles from well-known designers such as Joan Vass and Jean Marc, these clothes can be worn before, during and after pregnancy. Dresses, suits, sportswear and lingerie are designed to flatter the expectant woman. This successful national company has outfitted expectant actresses on "L.A. Law" and "Designing Women."

t. r. christian
925-5278

Setting a creative table is an art that can be accomplished through the expert advice and wide selection at t.r. christian. Villeroy & Boch, Christofle, Rosenthal, Chase, Lalique, Baccarat and all the best names in china, silver, crystal and accessories are available here. Traditional to contemporary is spiced up with classy accents.

Fawbush's
922-5717

They care about their customers. Owner Ginny Fawbush has a talent for selecting clothing and accessories that are high fashion, comfortable and easy-care. This is truly fantastic merchandise at reasonable to high prices. Great collection of costume jewelry. Also at Calhoun Square (825-3458).

Caroll of Paris
925-4065

Directly from France, where it is known for colorful, decorative knits, Caroll of Paris brings a European look to the Twin Cities. This dazzling collection of knitwear, much of it made in Italy, provides rich hues and expert craftsmanship to each garment.

A Touch of Glass
920-4222

The finest, most unusual crystal, china, flatware and stemware are presented in this beautiful place where everything sparkles. Collector enameled boxes and paperweights and an abundant display of marvelous jungle motif by Chase make a visit here an excursion.

Ataz
925-4883

An eclectic collection of handmade objects for home and garden. Birchbark, metal, wood, clay, fiber and stone, created by American craftsmen and blended with fine imported baskets, unusual textiles and antique furniture.

Bellini
920-2154

Heirlooms for a family to treasure for generations can be found at Bellini. They have the finest designer furniture for children in the world! Cribs, beds, dressers, chests and changing tables will make your child's room a wonderland of comfort and stimulation. The toys are chosen to help in the developmental stages of childhood and to improve dexterity and alertness. Mobiles, graphics and pictures do not just decorate the room but also stimulate the child.

H.O.B.O.
926-3034

There is a lively and tasteful mixture of women's fashion and casual clothing here. Owned by Richard Hinquist who enjoys a fine reputation and has quite a following, H.O.B.O. focuses on items that allow customers to create their own look.

Polly Berg
920-0183

Polly Berg is an oasis of femininity. In every selection, from china, linens and centerpieces to lingerie and loungewear by Fernando Sanchez, Christian Dior and Periphery, this couturier knows what appeals to discerning, decisive women. There are sachets, notecards, lucite bath accessories, monogrammed sheets, towels and bedding.

I. B. Diffusion
927-8131

This shop is headquarters for one of the most colorful women's clothing lines in the country. Knit sweaters and coats in colors that are really vivid are the specialty of I.B. Diffusion. Cotton and wool blends, silks and denim are decorated with beads, applique, color blocks and facet-cut glass. Stirrup pants, silk shirts, city shorts, T-shirts and knit pants add to this powerful and appealing collection.

Accents
922-3674

Every little detail that will enhance your best look can be found in this ultimate accessories shop. Unique clothing items, scarves, hair ornaments, hats, hosiery, handbags, Lancome beauty products, belts and jewelry of the most sumptuous kind fill every nook and cranny.

Games by James
925-9656

For family fun, intellectual stimulation and competitive play, a game from Games by James is a buy that has lasting value. They are up on what is new and what will pique customer interest. James knows that people want to use leisure time wisely so they have assembled an inventory of board games, puzzles, cards, and card-playing accoutrements that keeps the metro area thinking, guessing, betting and cheering. A unique feature of the Galleria store is the Create-a-Book service that makes personalized children's storybooks on the computer. There are five stores in the Twin Cities and Games by James is in Rochester too.

Bockstruck's
929-3143

Along with tennis bracelets and necklaces, the world's leading jewelry, watch and gem designers are on display at Bockstruck's. Their collection includes the most valuable and distinctive jewelry and gems in the international market. Priceless stones and fine metals from Jose Hess, pearls from Mikimoto and watches by Rolex and Movado are on hand at this beautiful store.

Signature
925-5215

Remembering that a hand-written letter and a greeting card with a heart-felt note are the nicest gifts, Signature has selected the best in writing instruments, greeting cards and stationery. Pens by Mont Blanc, Waterman and Cross and a large inventory of personally selected gifts make Signature an important outlet for the better basics of life. Glass animals, music boxes, desk accessories, photo albums and other amenities are constantly being updated at this smart shop.

France Avenue is a boulevard of shopping opportunity. Leisure Lane, Brandon Square, Yorktown Fashion Mall and Centennial Lakes Plaza are less pricey than Galleria and add to the endless consumer choices.

LAKE MINNETONKA AREA

Lake Minnetonka is the grand mistress of metro area waterways. Its size and splendor have brought to its shores Minnesota's wealthiest families and most opulent estates. The numerous bays and inlets are filled with people of all stripes and interests who cannot resist the allure of the lake.

WAYZATA
Zip Code 55391

Nestled on the northeast corner of Lake Minnetonka, twelve miles west of downtown Minneapolis, is Wayzata. Founded in 1854, Wayzata is a mecca of unique and high quality specialty shopping. There are a half dozen shopping centers in Wayzata. We will highlight some of the stores in each center and leave some for exploration. Shopping can be exhausting and Wayzata abounds with inviting places to relax and refresh. Restaurants are everywhere. **Sunsets** (473-5253) and **Sasha's** (475-3354) overlook the lake and offer outdoor dining. Either the distinguished **Blue Point** (475-3636), which specializes in seafood, or the cozy **Wayzata Bay Tea Room** (476-8120) can provide a quiet respite. Running through the center of the Wayzata shopping district, Wayzata Boulevard houses numerous eating spots including Perkins, Country Kitchen, McDonalds, Kentucky Fried Chicken and Burger King. One of the few remaining Bridgeman's is located in the Wayzata Bay Center. Adding to Wayzata's Currier and Ives look, a trolley car circles the city's retail areas during warm weather and is available for private rental (473-9595). The picturesque Wayzata Depot on Lake Street is a remnant of the city's past. Holiday shopping in Wayzata is festive with Madrigal singers, hot cider and ice skating on the lake.

Bird Feed Store
15710 Wayzata Boulevard
473-4283

"Feed the birds, tuppence a bag." The lore and thrill of feeding the birds is brought to life here. Specializing in the nutritional needs of all birds -- domestic and wild -- a variety of seeds, sweet cakes, drilled corn trees and a zillion kinds of feeders are available. Equipment for fending off squirrels and varmints is also available.

Gerrings Car Wash
1405 East Wayzata Boulevard
473-4535

Luxury at the car wash makes Gerring's a priceless addition to Wayzata's Lake Street. Gerrings features Mario Andretti's Hanna wash process. Your car is vacuumed, cleaned and polished -- inside and out -- and hand dried while you wait in a clean glassed-in room, sip coffee or a soda and watch the transformation. A first class operation! Allow 15 minutes and budget a minimum of $8.95 plus tax.

Down in the Valley
1147 East Wayzata Boulevard
473-7442

Down in the Valley is a well-rounded outlet for compact discs and tapes. They carry a good representation of all musical styles and artists including rock, folk, new age, jazz and classical. Interspersed among the great selection of popular titles is the unusual and the esoteric. Down in the Valley has sales with as much as a 25% discount on classical CD's. A classy deal. Also in Richfield (869-0978) and two stores in Golden Valley (544-0033), one of which is totally devoted to used CDs, LPs and tapes (544-1375).

Ski Hut Sporting Goods
1175 East Wayzata Boulevard
473-8843

A leader in ski equipment and clothing, Ski Hut handles Volkl and Solomon skis. Their clothing lines include Columbia, Obermeyer, Spyder and Bogner. This shop is an authority in the area on every aspect of skiing from consultation to equipment. They have year-round clothing and Skurfer ski boards to pull behind boats.

THE WAYZATA HOME CENTER
1250 East Wayzata Boulevard

If you are seriously interested in re-doing your home or just browsing, take your time to examine and savor the variety of tastes and styles found within The Wayzata Home Center. Decorating and home care are the main attractions at The Home Center.

MJ Galleries
449-0954

Original oils and high quality reproductions of traditional, European and old world subject matter. Ornate frames adorn all paintings including dog and hunts scenes and elaborate botanical scenes.

Bona Celina
449-0377

Look like a million bucks! Designer goods, including Carlisle dresses and suits, are offered by owner Dorothy Pedersen. She showcases consignment clothing as well as a few new pieces in her small shop. Prices are reasonable and goods are quality.

Memories
473-3123

"London, Paris, Wayzata" is not an idle boast for Memories antiques. Unusual European and classic American furnishings of enormous size and extravagance fill the shop. Each display is beautifully offset by dazzling accessories and opulent detail. The bedroom suites are grand and romantic and seem to disappear quickly. Crystal chandeliers and wall sconces are in abundance, armoires suitable as entertainment centers or bars, linen presses, gentleman's dressers and ornate day beds fill this stylish shop. Owners Howard and Bob never run out of lively conversation or fresh coffee and have an amazing knack for finding just about any item you may want or dream of. They know the antique market in America and can bring its best to you. Also in Eden Prairie (941-0252).

An Elegant Place
449-9505

Outfit your life with the finer things, the essential and the elegant. Antique wicker, new and antique linens, jewelry and gifts. Reproductions of antique buggies are popular with doll collectors. Among their treasures are tiny, heart-shaped china tooth fairy boxes.

Great Reflections
476-6384

Brighten, enliven, reflect! So you've found an armoire you want to convert to a bar or a display case?! Owners Darrell Miller and Beth Anderson can mirror the inside, install glass doors and light the interior to create a showstopper. They also mirror walls, doors, do custom-framed mirrors, glass shelves, table tops, shower doors, and a variety of other reflective work. Great Reflections can expand and brighten your world.

The Corner Door
473-2274

Owner Joyce Webster and her executive helpers Myrna, Terry, Eunice, Jean and Ken love to welcome you to their ever-changing collection of consignment home furnishings. Here you can find the unexpected any time you visit. In business 23 years and experienced in converting unwanted goods into cash for their consignors, you can always plan on a laugh and on being "up" after a stop here, whether or not you've made a purchase.

Serendipity
476-8285

Vicki Johanneck shares her love of old and new dolls, bears and Barbies in this delightful spot. She buys, sells and trades and has a wealth of information about shows and sales of interest to collectors.

Orvis-Gokey
785 East Lake Street
475-2475

Made for the outdoor people, Orvis-Gokey carries exclusively the Orvis label of clothing for women and men. This very distinctive and wholesome look can be found from head to toe including Gokey footwear which is made in St. Paul. They are also fly fishing specialists and hunting outfitters. Luggage in the Gokey and Orvis labels can be found as well as books on the great outdoors.

Silver Creek Design Studio
755 East Lake Street
475-2211

The "Better Homes & Gardens" set hangs out here. Handsome new furniture and accessories are displayed in traditional settings. Nettle Creek bedspreads, several fabric lines, floor and wall coverings and window treatments are available. Smart mirrors, lamps, display cabinets and desks are for sale and decorating assistance is available from a qualified staff.

Jan's of Wayzata
765 East Lake Street
473-0747

Jan's has an ingenuity for presenting women's clothing with a strong fashion emphasis. Labels such as St. John Knits, Geiger, Jones New York, Albert Nipon and William Pearson grace this jaunty shop. They carry a wide range of better to designer brands. Nice accessories including jewelry and handbags.

P.O.S.H.
743 East Lake Street
473-2594

An outstanding collection of traditional and contemporary household furnishings and accessories from napkin rings to room dividers and dried floral arrangements. The approach here is a daring one that asks clients to risk making bold statements in home furnishings. Dramatic pieces that will add distinction to your home.

The Traveling Collector
733 East Lake Street
473-9310

Their pride and joy is the unusual and exotic. Because their inventory is collected from around the world you are not going to find run-of-the-mill goods here. Colorful and whimsical jewelry, mirrors, garden statuary, satchels and vests made from Turkish rugs, silly and tempting art and gadgets.

The Gold Mine
332 South Broadway
473-7719

Warning! Wear your dark glasses! The Gold Mine is blinding with silver and crystaline splendor. Here they can promise elegance and history in home furnishings and every piece of china, crystal, sterling and jewelry consigned by Minnesota's finest families. The multi-owner shop appraises antiques and conducts estate sales. This place is a must.

Wayzata Mail Center
326 South Broadway
475-1602

After you've blown the family fortune and lavished your excesses in wondrous Wayzata, you'll want to send your booty home. The Mail Center wraps and ships anywhere, sells gift wrap, cartons and packaging supplies, offers photo copying, fax and Western Union money transfers. What could be handier?

WAYZATA MARQUEE PLACE

Colorful festive shops on the main stretch of Lake Minnetonka waterfront invite shoppers to Marquee Place. The Refreshment Trolley, parked on the sidewalk, is a sign of the mood here -- a leisurely place to browse or buy.

Talbots (473-1164), with its bright red door and fine array of women's apparel, sets the stage at Marquee Place. They make shopping a pageant affair.

Neighbors include **Salon Marquee** (473-3768) and **Rodica Facial Salon** (475-3111). **Latham Optical** (476-4185) can complete your self-care. Before you leave the neighborhood, relax at the **Wayzata Tea Room** (476-8120) for a cup of country tea.

Menswear with a traditional style or with a touch of the country club and the nautical life is ever present at **Sims, Ltd.** (473-4633). Their Ivy League/East coast look is well done. The madras shorts and shirts last forever. **Chico's** (476-1812) is presented elsewhere in this book.

Some of the other spots we love are:

Hurricane
475-1155

Sailor Heaven! All sorts of nautical gear for men and women. You can equip yourself for foul weather or the sun and the calm seas here, whether on deck or at the dock. Sailing related cards, gifts and amusing accessories.

Blanc de Blanc
691 Lake Street
473-8275

Everything in this immaculate and tasteful space is white or near-white. A variety of products in different price ranges, including hand made jewelry, baby clothes, bedding and gifts galore, garden and Bar-B-Q items, lucite accessories, kitchen gadgets, exquisite towels and linens all make Blanc de Blanc a safe haven when you need a wedding, hostess or shower gift. Complimentary gift wrapping includes a white feather, adding the touch of class you would expect from this marvelous shop.

Emerald Evenings
683 East Lake Street
473-1543

Emerald Evenings is a small elegant shop with racks full of one-of-a-kind designer dresses retailing from $200 to $2,500 which may be rented for $50 to $250. Evening gowns and cocktail dresses dripping with pearls and sequins are here -- lace, velvet, satin, silk -- all set to take you to the Symphony Ball, a beauty pageant, your neighbor's dinner party or to make you a drop-dead mother-of-the-bride.

The Side Door
Marquee Place
473-1937

When you shop The Side Door you won't see yourself coming and going because their designer fashions are purchased in small quantities. Unique handbags, scarves, shoes and wonderful jewelry complete the look. Service is personal and wardrobe planning and coordinating are available. Generally the sale racks hold super buys.

Brian L. Walters, Goldsmith
641 East Lake Street, Suite 208
475-3505

In the heart of Wayzata, there is Brian Walters, Goldsmith, purveyor of art and gems. In his design studio above Talbots, Brian has been personalizing designs of diamonds and gemstones for 17 years. He also does appraisals and repairs on the premises. Open six days a week, Brian welcomes evening appointments if more convenient for his customers.

The Bookcase
607 Lake Street
473-8341

This is an extraordinary bookstore specializing in personal attention. No matter what your needs, the helpful staff is happy to assist. Children's books and hostess gifts are found alongside best-sellers. Personal requests are no trouble and a special joy seems to guide each out-of-print search. Gift certificates are available. The Bookcase will gift wrap and mail. Fine stationery by Crane as well as a selection of note and greeting cards. There is a complete line of leatherbound English date and address books, guest books and trip log/diaries.

P.O.S.H. Pantry
324 Manitoba Avenue South
475-2423

No detail is overlooked in this classy shop. Unique tabletop accessories, kitchen and bath items, linens, gourmet food and custom gift baskets. The best snack crackers anywhere, Neva Betta, are sugar-free, cholesterol-free and wonderful with their jams and jellies. If you are searching for a hostess gift, P.O.S.H. pantry will provide the unique items you know are out there somewhere.

Five Swans
309 East Lake Street
473-4685

Design and function meet in Five Swan's collection of china, cookware, crystal. Each display sparkles and beckons. For the gifts you can't find anywhere else, Five Swans is your answer. Bridal registry and complimentary gift wrap.

Across the street from Five Swans is Sasha's Deli and Grill, The Depot and, heading back to town, Sunsets and Wuollet Bakery. Then...

The Wayzata Children's Shop
800 East Lake Street
473-2575

Patronized by discriminating customers seeking better quality clothing for girls (sizes infant to pre-teen) and boys (sizes infant through 20), the Wayzata Children's Shop is a community mainstay. In addition to clothing, educational toys and games are available as well as accessories and infant bedding. A great spot for gifts. The selection is extensive and gift wrap is complimentary.

THE VILLAGE SHOPS
800 Block of East Lake Street

Neatly lined up under Victorian towers and turrets at the east end of town are The Village Shops. **Hunter's Glen** (473-3398) is a good spot for soup, a sandwich and talk, talk, talk! There's also a **McGlynn's Bakery** outlet store. You'll be attracted to The Village Shops by the variety of merchandise and the easy access. Our favorite stores are **Lake Street Papery, Inc.** and **Bone Adventure.**

Bone Adventure
812 East Lake Street
473-0227

Mpls/St. Paul Magazine votes Bone Adventure the Twin Cities' best pet clothing store. And no wonder! Where else do Canine Klein, Oscar de la Rawhide, Ruff Lauren and Puppy Ellis proudly display their creations? There are leather coats, raincoats, boots, life jackets and sweaters, rhinestone-studded collars, rawhide pizzas and more in Cathy and Brian Fulmer's shop. Pet grooming is done on the premises and boarding is available. Also in Edina (920-2201).

Lake Street Papery, Inc.
866 East Lake Street
473-5647

Here you'll find terrific gift wrap, bags, ribbons, boxes and bows. Cards for every occasion, helium balloons, party supplies, wedding and social stationery, seasonal holiday items and gifts abound.

McGlynn's Bakery Outlet Store
840 East Lake Street
449-0516

Suitable for the kids' after-school snack or for a grand soiree, McGlynn's Bakery Outlets have both baked and frozen goods. Breads and rolls, croissants, cookies, pies, sweet rolls and donuts are discounted. Special entertaining may call for their tasty pies or cakes. The selection of tortes includes Chocolate Amaretto, Bavarian Raspberry and Bailey's Irish Cream. Also in Eden Prairie (934-5891) and Bloomington (881-6581).

WAYZATA BAY CENTER
900 Block of East Lake Street

Located at the intersection of Lake Street and County Road 15 in the heart of Wayzata is the area's largest shopping complex, surrounded by convenient free parking. A signboard at the center's entrance announces the many community activities which take place within the enclosed mall area -- antique shows, holiday entertainment and craft displays.

The Foursome Department Store is the place to go for just about any clothing need. The Foursome has five different shops:

Foursome Family: 473-4667

Foursome Family Shoe Store: 473-1556

Foursome Tall Men's Store: 473-2596

Foursome Ladies' Store: 473-2526

Foursome For Children: 473-0124

Bob's Shoe Repair
473-8248

The best shoe repair in the western suburbs and the nicest people to deal with when the dog has destroyed your favorite pump and you <u>have</u> to have it restored. Bob Fisher and his staff are miracle workers! The shop stocks every kind and color of shoe polish and creme, every length of shoelace imaginable and every footwear accessory you'll ever want.

Anderson's China
475-3444

Set an absolutely stunning table with Wedgwood, Herend, Spode, Royal Doulton, or Lenox and silver at everyday low prices from Gorham, Lunt, and Reed and Barton. Accent with Waterford, Orrefors or St. Louis crystal. Brides who register receive special "perks". This family owned purveyor of authentic quality has served the Upper Midwest for 112 years. Be assured that Anderson's can provide the tasteful ambiance that will charm your guests and distinguish your hospitality.

Picture This Framed
476-4205

This is not just another frame shop. Their selection stretches for miles and genial service abounds in this most reasonably priced shop. Owner Don Colpitts has been in this business since 1987 and has established a loyal following of patrons whose homes display his ingenious craftsmanship.

Androli Hair Designers
473-2503

"The Total Salon" serves contemporary and traditional tastes. Jerry Androli oversees his expert staff of designers, colorists, permanent wave technicians, manicurists and pedicurists. Full and mini facials, make-up lessons and application of professional hair and beauty products are available. Dan Hendrickson is probably the best color specialist in the Twin Cities and hangs his hat here. A second shop is located at 30 Water Street, Excelsior (470-0102). Here, too, Androli's furnishes progressive style.

DEEPHAVEN
Zip Code 55391

In the midst of Minnetonka is the small and inviting community of Deephaven. Just off the lake, Deephaven has winding streets, lovely homes and a "hidden away" atmosphere. There are a few shops in Deephaven that are worth looking into. **Carrol Shepherd's Consignment Shop** and **Deephaven Antiques** are both in this area and are presented in the "Antiques" section of this book.

One More Time
18312 Minnetonka Boulevard
476-0894

One More Time is the answer for parents who want to provide their children the amenities of growing up without paying retail prices. This consignment shop has children's used toys and furniture that are well cared for and reasonably priced. Cribs, high chairs, car seats, strollers and many, many accessories are sold. The book and toy collection has the best of everything. Owner Nan Kangas is very fussy and accepts only quality goods.

Bumbershute
18304 Minnetonka Boulevard
475-2684

Extremely stylish and up-to-date women's clothing is available at this upscale boutique. Casual wear, day and evening suits, interesting accessories in jewelry and handbags are selected with a flair for the dramatic.

Ultimate Function
18202 Minnetonka Boulevard
475-3088

The ultimate function is people getting together for a good time and this shop makes it possible. The huge balloons in brilliant colors with streamers that travel to the moon are the best around. Paper dishes and napkins, tablecloths and utensils that coordinate around color or theme will give your event a festive air. There are also wild clothing items such as baseball caps with flamingos atop, 3-D T-shirts and sweatshirts and outrageous sunglasses and jewelry. Everything that decorates your life is here.

Sugarbakers
18160 Minnetonka Boulevard
473-8749

This is a complete and lavish gallery of furnishings and design expertise. Opulent overstuffed furniture and rich accent pieces such as chests and boxes, Chinese garden seats, lamps, mirrors and prints. Fabrics of every imagination are available to adorn furniture lines from Pearson, Land and Pennsylvania Classics. The design service is complimentary.

Heritage Clock Shop
3424 Highway 101
475-1489

Heritage has clocks that will become part of your family legacy including Sligh, Howard Miller and New England grandfather clocks. A wide variety of wall and table clocks, too.

EXCELSIOR
Zip Code 55331

This city on the lake attracts people of all ages and interests and is one of the metro area's most popular gathering spots. The allure of the lake and the open country feeling have brought to Excelsior people who enjoy the restaurants, shops, boutiques, entertainment, recreation and services that fill this active city. The main business district of Excelsior is centered on Water Street running from the south shore of Lake Minnetonka. The street is known for progressive retailing and fascinating merchandise. Gifts, arts and crafts, antiques, clothing, furniture and the practical and necessary things of life are seen in this busy and informal district. You'll want to take in a play at **The Old Log Theater** (474-5951) and maybe a cruise on **The Queen of Excelsior** (474-2502). And people come from miles around to take advantage of the good movies and low ticket price at the Excelsior **Dock.**

EXCELSIOR MILL

A turn-of-the-century lumber mill now houses four wonderful shops filled with gifts and accessories featuring homespun elegance and contemporary sophistication.

Provisions
320 Water Street
474-6953

Provisions has life's necessities in practical and opulent forms. Kitchen gadgets, cookbooks of all persuasions, inexpensive glassware, mixing bowls, insulated baking sheets, picnic gear, and gourmet foods, including hard-to-find spices, and sauce mixes. The shop offers the complete line of Crabtree and Evelyn toiletries and Portmerion's magnificent Pomona, Birds of Britain and Botanic Garden china. Provisions offers a fabulous selection of paper products, including Caspari and Haut Papier. This shop is bursting with hostess gifts, oil lamps, trays, metal baskets, coasters, pitchers. The biggest decision you'll have to make is when to stop the buying. It's all so tempting. Provisions has an excellent sale section.

The Sampler
314 Water Street
474-4794

Don't pass by The Sampler because you don't sew. They are devoted to making your home a better place for people whether you do it all yourself, ask for help or buy ready-made. This quilt and needlework shop has great ideas for the craftsperson and for those who would like to be. Classes are taught in such subjects as smocking, rug hooking, doll making and Battenberg lace.

The Sign of the Eagle
312 Water Street
474-2315

This shop oozes small town ambiance and is filled with new country furniture. In this simple atmosphere, there are lamps, prints, woodware, table linens, dinnerware (including Rowe pottery) and spatterware. There is an abundance of pewter, collectible holiday ornaments and reproductions of old-fashioned signs. Cotton Afghans in traditional coverlet patterns, plaids, hunt, village and sampler scenes, are exceptionally nice items.

D.B. & Company
310 Water Street
474-7428

Treat yourself to a bag of popcorn, some fancy candy or a cup of coffee and wander through five rooms of fun and fascination. Country items abound. English lace-trimmed pillows, tissue box covers, jewel boxes, baskets trimmed with bows and berries, baby gifts, mobiles, toiletries in every imaginable motif or pattern. There's a room dedicated to Minnesota which is filled with the silly such as bird houses for mosquitoes and the serious such as pine benches and shelves. At Christmas time, the prettiest topiaries are here, snapped up as quickly as they appear.

Continuing down the street . . .

Once Upon A Time
369 George Street
470-0390

Antique hunting can be a mini-vacation at Once Upon A Time. The pleasure of a Victorian house filled with the aroma of potpourri and the charm of heirloom furnishings takes customers to another time and place. Antiques are tastefully displayed.

Gray Gardens
366 Water Street
474-9150

This family of artists and craftsmen have the technical skill and the aesthetic flair to make any project a major triumph. In this charming old house antiques are interspersed with fresh flowers and greenery. The Kruger family includes Matthew, the floral design expert, Andrew, the landscape contractor, Konrad, the photographer and William, a remodeling/construction expert. They pool their ideas to give you the country look.

Kidding Around
347 Water Street
470-5087

Why would you buy kids' clothes anyplace else? With the way little ones grow out of their clothing, resale clothes are the ticket for the frugal and fashion conscious parent. Kidding Around buys and sells clean, quality, brand name clothes, toys and baby equipment. They like kids and they show it with their caring approach to making them look good.

Artworks Art & Frame, Inc.
345 Water Street
474-5000

Preserve your pictures and art pieces and display them proudly in your home. The artistic and knowledgeable staff will assist in designing mats and frames that will enhance any work of art. Artworks is also the area headquarters for artist's materials.

Water Street Clothing Co.
287 Water Street
474-0474

This is "knock 'em dead" fashion with the greatest personal attention to your needs and wishes. You will not see yourself coming and going with Water Street Clothing. Fabrics, colors, designs are original and made for the woman with class and confidence. Also Galleria (927-6336).

Mary O'Neal & Co.
217 Water Street
470-0205

O'Neal & Co. offers quality crystal, china, fine art and accessories. Their breakfronts, sofas and tables are handsome. They will buy outright or consign, and they manage estate and moving sales.

The Doll Buggy
234 Water Street
474-1861

Don't you just want to take one home with you? Owner Carolyn Larsen sells gorgeous dolls, cute dolls, real dolls and fantastic dolls to make this place seem like the best childhood dream. Doll accessories are available too.

Mary Ellen Bartholow
4700 Fatima Place
474-8764

This is where dolls come from and where they go when they need a friend. Mary Ellen understands dolls and the people who care for them. She applies technical skills and tender, loving care to doll repair. She makes enchanting stuffed dolls and designs and sews doll clothing.

Frog Island Bookstore
50 Water Street
474-7612

Wonderful books for the entire family. They welcome special orders and always gift wrap free. Service is their specialty.

Heritage II
36 Water Street
474-1231

Featuring Scandinavian and British Isle imports, Heritage II has crystal, dinnerware, stainless, teak gifts, candles, cards, sweaters, hats, ties, clogs, linens, soaps, jewelry, flags. They have a bridal registry. Also White Bear Lake (429-4541).

Androli Hair Designers
30 Water Street
470-0102

Androli's is not only a salon but an institution in the local hair and beauty industry. The main shop in Wayzata is complemented by the Excelsior store. Their progressive brand of hair and skin care continues to lead the market. They know the latest trends, but their main goal is the best look for each client.

Antiquity Rose
Rose's Tea Room
429 Second Street
474-2661

Rose's is a funky little spot offering home cooking and antiques. If you like the table you're dining at or the picture on the wall, buy it! Everything in the place is for sale. You'll find china, silver, linens, jewelry -- and up the narrow staircase are two rooms generally bulging with children's furniture and a closet full of vintage clothing.

Kuempel Custom Clockmakers and Repair
21195 Minnetonka Boulevard
474-6177

For 65 years Kuempel clocks have been gracing homes, large and small, throughout the metro area. They have a history of pride and workmanship that makes their every piece a treasured possession. They will build clocks to the customer's wishes including grandfather, wall clocks and mantel clocks.

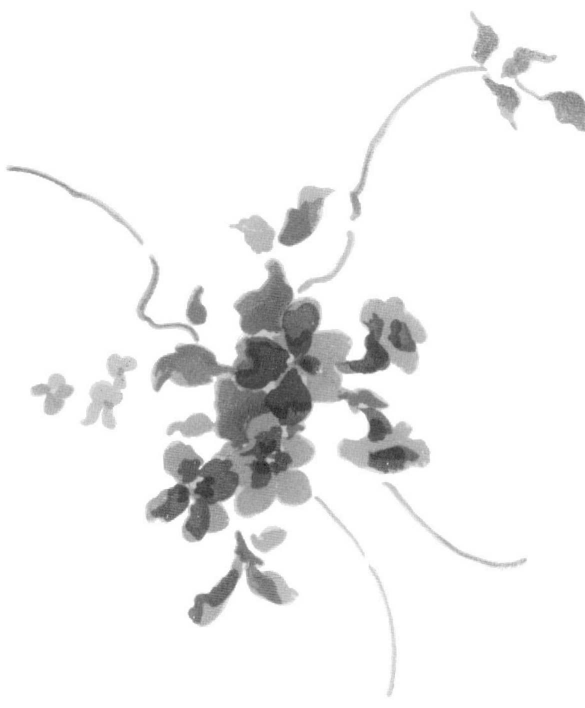

ART GALLERIES/MUSEUMS

MUSEUM GIFT SHOPS

American Swedish Institute
2600 Park Avenue
Minneapolis 55407
871-4907

The gift shop of this center of Swedish culture in America brims with the flavor of Sweden. China and glassware, linen and weavings, sweaters, wall hangings, books as well as Swedish art and crafts of many kinds are available.

Children's Museum
1217 Bandana Boulevard North
St. Paul 55108
644-5305

Everything in the gift shop at the Children's Museum is made to stimulate, entertain or educate children. Like the hands-on concept of the museum, the gifts give children the chance to experience a part of the environment.

Minnesota Museum of Art
Landmark Center, 5th at Market
St. Paul 55102
292-4355

The Landmarket gift shop of the Minnesota Museum of Art is located in Landmark Center.

Science Museum of Minnesota
30 East 10th Street
St. Paul 55101
221-9488

There are three shops in the Science Museum: the Explore Store, the Children's Explore and the Science Explore Store. All shops carry the wonder and magic of science in books, games, arts and crafts.

C. G. Rein Galleries
3523 West 76th Street
Edina 55435
927-4331

Artists with national reputations such as Jerome Tupa, Mary Jane Schmidt and Cha are sold and leased at this gallery which handles varied media. Contemporary paintings, sculpture, serigraphs, lithographs and woodcuts are among the outstanding art available at C. G. Rein.

Dolly Fiterman Fine Arts
100 University Avenue S.E.
Minneapolis 55414
Phone: 623-3300

Newly housed in the former Pillsbury Library, Dolly Fiterman continues to present major contemporary American and European artists, including some of the best of the regional artists. The work ranges from quiet, delicate florals to the most startling avant-garde.

elayne
6111 Excelsior Boulevard
Minneapolis 55416
926-1511

One of the widest selections of quality art is found at elayne gallery. The foremost contemporary artists including Peter Max, LeRoy Neiman, Mark King, Tomia DePaola and Altman. Periodic sales at excellent prices on both art works and framing keep elayne very competitive in the local retail art market.

The Guthrie Theater
725 Vinland Place
Minneapolis 55403
347-1167

The art, jewelry and music that will make memorable performances a part of your life long after the curtain has closed are found in the Guthrie Gift Shop.

Minneapolis Institute of Arts
2400 - 3rd Avenue South
Minneapolis 55406
870-3131
870-3200 recorded message regarding open hours and exhibitions

One of the finest art museums in the country, the Minneapolis Institute of Arts has an extensive and renowned collection. In addition to the museum, the Institute offers an educational program that reaches all corners of the state. Admission is free, except for very special exhibitions. The Museum Shop features jewelry and gift items from around the world, including many products adapted from pieces in their own permanent collection as well as from the collections of many museums nationwide. Operated by volunteers, the Shop's proceeds go directly to the support of the Museum.

On the first Friday of each month, with the exception of July, the Institute hosts an Expertise Clinic and invites you, at no charge, to bring in art and objects for which their curators may provide historical background.

The Walker Art Center Book Shop
725 Vineland Place
Minneapolis 55403
375-7622

Art books, magazines, jewelry, toys, notecards, postcards, posters and T-shirts make lively, artistic statements.

ANTIQUES

The antique and collector shops featured in SHOPPING THE TWIN CITIES . . . and more have been selected for their distinction. They truly represent the goods from the past that are valuable and stylish.

Most antique stores are closed one or two days each week, often Mondays or Tuesdays. Their hours vary, sometimes by season. Some are open only by appointment. It pays to call in advance.

Great River Antiques
210 - 3rd Avenue North
Minneapolis 55401
338-1109

The Warehouse District's most venerable collection, Great River Antiques is a wonderland of taste, subtlety and treasure. You enter a different world here. No wonder Whoopi Goldberg scrawled on the wall "I love this place." It is instantly infatuating in its display of silver, gilt, crystal, porcelain, classic and neoclassic furniture and period art. Visitors are astounded by the grandeur of major furniture pieces and authentic object d'art. The dealers at Great River are among the area's foremost antiquaries who have a self-imposed high standard of quality. They won't accept impostors and they don't want their clients to. If the splendor of Great River is too much and you need a break from the rigors of antiquing, step across the street to the Monte Carlo Bar and Grill for a meatloaf sandwich. So civil.

Cobweb Antiques
250 North Third Avenue
Minneapolis 55401
338-1315

This shop, a counterpoint to its grander Warehouse District neighbors, features classy junque and bibelot with surprises lurking in every corner. Don't be shocked to see a beautiful dining room suite right next to a collection of tin cans and tools. There is a spectacular collection of old lunch pails, 33, 45 and 78 phonograph records and a booth dedicated to left-handed people. There's no snobbery at Cobweb, but a quick and careful perusal may reveal the missing diadem, if not a cobweb or two.

Architectural Antiques
801 Washington Avenue North
Minneapolis 55401
332-8344

Named Twin Cities Best Home Decorating Store by Mpls/St. Paul Magazine, Architectural Antiques has saved a veritable fortune from the wrecking ball. The inventory here is of artifacts from dismantled and condemned buildings. You could reconstruct the homes of the past with their astounding array of everything from bath accessories, hardware, light fixtures/lamps, marble, brass, ironwork, railings, stained glass windows and doors, mailboxes, doorknockers, columns, pedestals, fireplace mantels and buffets. Even old street lights live here, waiting to be rediscovered and given new life. A fine selection of antique and reproduction garden statuary is offered here as well. Prices throughout the easily-browsed store are very reasonable and may be negotiated on big ticket items.

Lyndale House Antiques/Antiques Wholesale
2225 Lyndale Avenue South
Minneapolis 55405
871-3491

Purveyors and importers on a grand scale, Lyndale House has an enormous and ever-changing selection of British, European and American goods. They bring from the Continent container loads of select furniture pieces representing most styles and periods. Bedroom and dining suites, wardrobes and armoires, sideboards and bureaus, desks and cabinets of every imagination are regularly available. From Regency, Georgian, Victorian, Edwardian, art nouveau and art deco -- Lyndale House has a large collection of smaller items and specialize in unusual pieces.

H & B Gallery
2729 Hennepin Avenue South
Minneapolis 55408
874-6436

Superior quality and exquisite choice abound in this first-rate shop. 19th Century French gilt settee and matching chairs, a set of Aynsley china, antique bird prints, Russian icons and Currier & Ives are examples of stock. H & B has a gallery quality and can furnish your fantasies with authentic style.

Uptown Mall Antiques
1204 Lagoon Avenue South
Minneapolis 55408
827-3795

"Upbeat" is their motto and weird is their specialty. You'll find your lost dreams at Uptown at prices that make you smile. Thirty dealers are crowded into this hot pink building in the middle of the active Uptown area. They have a treasure trove of fifties memorabilia and surprising stock throughout.

**Bill Brantner's
Cobblestone Antiques™**
1010 West Lake Street
Minneapolis 55408
823-7373

Self-proclaimed as "Minnesota's Finest Antique Emporium," Cobblestone features a distinguished collection of silver, porcelain, oriental rugs, estate jewelry, prints, pottery, cut and art glass, American country, period and Victorian furniture, lighting fixtures and stained glass windows. Seventy professional dealers buy, sell, appraise and accept consignments in new, air conditioned surroundings. This is a reliable source of quality goods including important statement pieces and exquisite accessories.

Antiques Minnesota
1516 East Lake Street   1197 University Avenue West
Minneapolis 55407   St. Paul 55104
722-6000   646-0037

"Recycling America's Past" is an appropriate boast for this big and bountiful collection of quality goods. Five floors in the Lake Street store, filled with every piece of the past, provide the collector and the sentimentalist just what they're looking for at prices surprisingly modest.

China, glassware, silver, bric-a-brac, trinkets and oddities that tell the history of our state and nation make Antiques Minnesota an unsurpassed leader of the antique industry. Reproductions of antique hardware for drawers and cupboards are sold here also.

In the lower level of the Lake Street store, **The Lampmender** (722-LAMP) is located. They repair and refurbish all kinds of lamps and lighting fixtures. Glass shades, bulbs and hardware are sold. Also located in the lower level is **Antique Clock Repair** (722-9590), selling and repairing antique and new clocks. Antiques Minnesota offers china repair service that will rejuvenate broken or shattered pieces through undetectable craftsmanship.

ANTIQUE CORNER
West 50th Street and Xerxes South
Minneapolis 55410

This soup-to-nuts neighborhood is home to 11 dealers offering a myriad of styles, tastes, periods and values. Whether you're putting on the Ritz, furnishing a summer home or searching for museum-quality pieces, you're likely to find the answer at this collector's intersection. Be prepared for a marathon experience as you stroll from shop to shop in this busy retail area.

Park Avenue Antiques
4944 Xerxes Avenue South
922-0887

American and European goods, distinctive furniture, fine porcelain (Dresden, Sevres), art glass and pottery.

Antiques at Our House
3004 West 50th Street
926-5632

Large collection of Victorian furniture, oak, wicker and children's items.

American Classics Antiques
4944 Xerxes Avenue South
926-2509

Two floors loaded with pine, oak, wicker, country accessories, toys, advertising, small collectibles. Chair caning and wicker repair.

The Loft
5004-1/2 Xerxes Avenue South
922-4200

A tasteful hodgepodge of everything you'd find in an early 20th Century American home. Chair caning and refurbishing.

Yesteryears Appraisal Services
5004-1/2 Xerxes Avenue South
925-6181

Specializing in higher quality antiques and jewelry, distinctive estate pieces.

Eydie's Country Quilting Shop
2822 West 43rd Street
929-0645

Quilting supplies, 100% cotton fabrics, Amish quilts and rugs, antique accessories, classes.

Fjelde & Co. Antiques
3022 West 50th Street
922-7022

Eighteen rooms of country to Victorian, light fixtures, dried flowers, herbs.

Compliments
3014 West 50th Street
922-1702

American antiques and custom made furniture.

Yankee Peddler
5008 Xerxes Avenue South
926-1732

Specializing in lighting, furniture and accessories.

Treasures Antique Mall
1115 Excelsior Avenue East
Hopkins 55343
930-0477

Treasures is a curiosity shop of 9,000 square feet of antiques and collectibles, highlighted by a library of outstanding books on every aspect of antique collecting from costume jewelry to glassware and furniture.

Forty-five dealers offer a multitude of minute, mundane and majestic memorabilia. Art deco walking sticks, vintage magazines, fancy perfume bottles, delicate hair combs and pretty table appointments are in superabundance at Treasures. Some items are spectacular and pricey. Some inexpensive and irresistible. While in the neighborhood, stop at The Plastic Bag Mart, at 511 East Excelsior Boulevard, for the best deals around on plastic and paper products.

Mainstreet Antique Mall
901 Mainstreet
Hopkins 55343
931-9748

This place is just too much! Fifty dealers display military paraphernalia, deco pieces, 1920's jewelry, airline memorabilia and many unusual and bizarre items. Small pieces of our social and cultural history abound at Mainstreet Mall. Avoiding large items, the minutia of the past will take you on a sentimental and reasonably priced journey.

Capitol Arts & Antiques
134 East 9th Street
St. Paul 55101
227-3677

Capitol Arts has a 20 year reputation as buyer and seller of authentic 19th and 20th Century furnishings. They are avid students of the genre that include mission furniture, metalwork, art pottery and accessories from the American Arts & Crafts Movement. Their collection includes the works of Elbert Hubbard and Gustav Stickley. They are the area's prime source of Oriental and Navajo carpets and American and European paintings. Maintaining and rejuvenating quality pieces is as important at Capitol Arts & Antiques as procurement. Their extensive services include estate settlement, rug repair and dye bleeding removal, furniture restoration, art pottery, porcelain and cut glass repair, metalwork services, painting conservation and licensed appraisals. Specialized and discerning collectors and students of art and antiques seek Capitol as an expert source of merchandise and consultation.

French Antiques
174 West 7th Street
St. Paul 55102
293-0388

Here you'll not find grab bag merchandise. Owners Marc and Peggy Giunta travel to Europe, hand select and supervise the packing of their purchases. Their trips have been fruitful and have filled their St. Paul shop with authentic and significant pieces. For instance, one of their oldest pieces is an enormous circa-1705 Regency period walnut armoire with hand carved molding panels. By the sheer elegance and formality of style, the merchandise all appears grand. A Henry II style buffet, a Louis XIV mirrored armoire or styles known as "Chapeau de Gendarme" or "Parisienne" may seem formidable in the heartland, but with Marc and Peggy's counsel and concern, even the most pretentious piece can find a comfortable home.

Aladdin's Antique Alley
239 West 7th Street
St. Paul 55102
290-2981

Aladdin's is quaint and classy. They have gathered together a reputable stock of all kinds of antiques, large and small. The lost and forgotten effects of the past are rediscovered and look rather splendid here. The stairs that lead down to this lower-level shop set the mood for curious and clever collectible and antique china, glassware, brass, art, jewelry, furniture, advertising and paper goods.

John's Antiques
261 West 7th Street
St. Paul 55102
222-6131

John Remackel and Glen Anderson relish the old and choose with care their fine inventories. They have a general line of furniture and accessories with an emphasis on stylish pieces. They specialize in lighting fixtures, lamp parts and repair. John's Antiques adjoins Anderson's Lampshades. Both are a good stop.

Payne Avenue Antique Mall
1055 Payne Avenue
St. Paul 55106
772-1635

This is a collector's shop. The proprietors also own Mainstreet Mall in Hopkins and can aid any collectors's search for rare items. Advertising copy, vintage radios, beer collectibles, 50's artifacts, deco pieces, clocks and toys fill the wish list for specialty seekers. There are 67 dealers who have gathered under one roof treasured tidbits of the past.

Golden Lion Antiques
983 Payne Avenue
St. Paul 55101
778-1977

The Golden Lion collection is filled with classic and collectible antiques. European, American and Oriental glassware and furniture selected for the discriminating collector. Chinese painted chests, Louis XIV chairs, immigrant trunks, huge hand-embroidered Chinese tapestry and modest country primitives are among this rich collection.

Emporium Antiques
1037 Payne Avenue
St. Paul 55101
771-5002

Considered one of the preeminent dealerships in the Twin Cities, Emporium consistently provides authentic and distinctive antiques. The collection is worldwide and favors classic and imperial-style goods. French clocks, Egyptian cabinets, a Majolica urn, 18th Century paintings are included in this stunning collection.

J & E Antiques
1000 Arcade Street
St. Paul 55106
771-9654

J & E Antiques occupies a prominent position in one of the most prolific antique areas in the Twin Cities. This 20-year-old family business has 6,000 square feet of furniture including some spectacular pieces from the East Coast. There is also a large inventory of railroad memorabilia, political pens, brewiana, toys and advertising items.

Early Times Emporium
1882 Wayzata Boulevard
Long Lake 55356
473-9804

A glittering festival of glass and china, silver and porcelain are packed into this country shop. Early Times is headquarters for Depression Glass of every pattern and color as well as Heisey, Fiesta and delftware. Art works, miscellaneous primitives and collectibles and vintage furniture complete this massive representation of yesteryear.

Country School House Shops
5300 Highway 12
Maple Plain 55359
479-6353

It is truly reminiscent of good old golden rule days, this 1920's brick schoolhouse. Organized into shops with 100 dealers, School House is a fascinating museum and warehouse of antiquity. Furniture, fresh linens and laces, antique toys, Coca Cola artifacts, tack, jewelry, art primitives and classics. There are three floors of ordinary and unusual memorabilia. The numerous concessionaires bring their varied interest and tastes to an almost overwhelming display of quality merchandise.

Steeple Antiques
5310 Main Street
Maple Plain 55359
479-4375

A 100 year-old church is the perfect place to find a memory and visit history. From narthex to sanctuary, every crook and cranny is a display case of country and primitive goods, Victoriana, toys, tools, china, stoneware and linens. Amid the rolling hills of this horse country west of Minneapolis, Steeple offers competitive prices in a friendly small-town atmosphere. Quality consignments are accepted. Coffee and cookies are served to browsing customers.

Fraser Cameron
926-6609

This by appointment only vendor of antiques will introduce you to an exotic world of classic American and European goods. For connoisseurs of the elegant and the expensive, Fraser Cameron features French 17th, 18th and 19th Century clocks, vintage porcelains, paintings and furniture from England, Germany, France and the United States.

Gray's Bay Antiques
17232 Gray's Bay Boulevard
Minnetonka 55391
476-8510

Housed in a former neighborhood grocery store, Gray's Bay is brimming with charming traces of the past. From Victorian to deco, from respected titles to garden-variety fare, Gray's gives visitors a grand tour of 18th, 19th and 20th Centuries through furniture, silver, glassware, art, stoneware, primitives and modern collectibles. Fanciers of nautical scenes and subjects will admire their extensive collection of toy boats and sea and ship objects. The collection is eclectic, ranging from Steuben glass to large furniture pieces, including an enormous gun/fishing tackle case longing for a good home.

Carrol Shepherd's Consignment Shop
Deephaven Court
18285 Minnetonka Boulevard
Deephaven
473-1554

The inventory is as merry and magical as the proprietress herself and good deals are legend at Carrol Shepherd's. This shop is a maze of function and frippery from fine estates and crowded attics throughout the metro area. Carrol has an eye for lovely pieces and effusive decoration. She offers her wares with good advice and good humor. Her steady clientele have spread the word that amid the ever-changing inventory you'll find consistent quality and friendly atmosphere. Carrol's shop is just 2.7 miles west of Highway 494 and here you can not only purchase but also consign with confidence.

Deephaven Antiques
18348 Minnetonka Boulevard
Deephaven 55391
476-4334

The best of the past is abundant at Deephaven Antiques. Quality room appointments, new and estate jewelry, fine art and rare coins make Deephaven the province of the connoisseur. Each room is a studio arranged by genre. One is devoted to jewelry, another contains early American furnishings, another Art Deco. There are Oriental carpets, postcards, dolls, vintage clothing and linens, manuscripts, prints and ship's logs. Owner Graham Fonda is an appraiser with 20 years of experience and a 1,000 volume library of antique and collectible reference books. They do expert jewelry repair and estate sales.

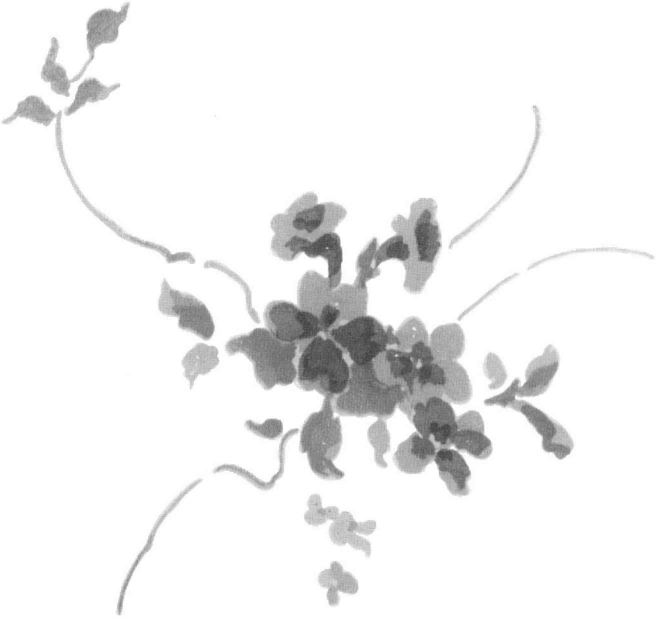

INTRODUCTION TO CONSIGNMENT SHOPS

You can be fabulous and frugal, or to borrow from Frances Moschino, "cheap and chic," by shopping the several quality consignment outlets in the metro area. With patience and an eye for value, the savvy shopper need not sacrifice style or quality. The metro area is seeing the rise of a new breed of upscale consignment shops that do not have the secondhand or rummage sale look. The discerning shopper will be able to find labels such as Kathryn Conover, Eileen West, Dior, Calvin Klein, Ferragamo, Gucci and Coach on local consignment store shelves. In a society that changes careers and attitudes frequently, wardrobes quickly become obsolete and a market for recycled clothing has developed. The image of the consignment shop has changed. They are not the haunts of the down-and-out but rather the milieu of professional people and style mavens. Shop owners have developed strict standards for the merchandise they will accept to reduce the "Second-hand Rose" image.

Designer Wardrobe
6628 Penn Avenue South
Richfield 55423
861-1460

This resale boutique is an excellent source of quality women's apparel. Seasonal wardrobes, coats, furs, handbags, shoes, jewelry, belts and hats are accepted with a strict eye for quality and style.

Elsie's Closet
3105 Nicollet Avenue South
Minneapolis 55408
825-5627

Owner Elsie Iverson buys her merchandise at local estate sales and has a smashing assemblage of vintage and costume clothing. She recently provided hats, shoes, dresses, blouses, scarfs and gloves for the motion picture "Blaze."

Encore
8787 Columbine Road
Anderson Lakes Parkway & 169
Eden Prairie 55344
944-9290

Sizes, shapes and styles for all occasions are found at this consignment shop. You can turn your clothing into cash and step out in style at Encore. They also have sample lines and some new items.

The Pink Closet
4024 East 46th Street
Minneapolis 55406
724-2468

The cream of local consignments shops, The Pink Closet offers designer goods and overall quality clothing at a fraction of the original cost. In addition to a wide selection of women's apparel, The Pink Closet is the leader in men's consignment clothing. Suits and sportcoats of every size and style, Ralph Lauren wool-lined denim jackets and an ever-changing selection of high quality men's wear make The Pink Closet the undisputed consignment leader. Imagine a brand new Bottega Veneta purse for $18! They ask, "Why pay more?" We say ditto!

Repeat Performance
707 West 34th Street
Minneapolis 55408
824-3035

Spiffy and stylish 40's and 50's outfits make Repeat Performance a crown jewel of the vintage clothing market. Sandy Whiteford, owner, shops estate sales and furnishes a look with flare and authenticity.

Rodeo Drive
4110 Minnetonka Boulevard
St. Louis Park 55416
920-0188

Top quality designer clothing from Ralph Lauren, Anne Klein, Donna Karan, Claiborne, Joan Voss, Ellen Tracy and a host of other acclaimed designers abound in this general, upbeat store. Dramatic jewelry pieces and fabulous debut gowns are available at moderate prices. Rodeo Drive is accepting men's clothes too.

Zelda Z's
721 Winnetka Avenue North
Golden Valley 55427
541-0818

Zelda's is where you might find that prized item, that longed-for look, that hoped-for piece at unbelievable prices. Pricey designer labels and standard apparel items are the menu here.

OFF-THE-BEATEN-PATH SHOPS

Byerly's
Eight Twin Cities locations

This is the piece de resistance of supermarkets, the Taj Mahal of grocery stores. Byerly's have set an industry standard by their vast arrays of food items and sumptuous amenities presented in Epicurean elegance. The quality and quantity of their groceries is matched by their steadfast customer service. No quirk of taste or specialty of menu is unfulfilled. Their home economists advise customers on every aspect of food choice and preparation.

The flagship of their operation is the St. Louis Park store where the Gallery presents porcelain, china, crystal and furniture from European and Oriental markets. The selection includes Lalique, Baccarat, Boehm, Caithness of Scotland, Herend, Judith Lieber. All-in-all, this outlet is more like Tiffany's than the A&P.

All stores have large deli and bakery departments and catering services. The popular Leann Chin Chinese cuisine is available as well as their own estimable menu. Ever the progressive entrepreneur, Byerly's accepts Visa and Mastercard as just one more customer convenience.

Lunds
Eight Twin Cities locations

The folks at Lunds have an absolute mania for customer service. They will shelter you from the elements, help plan your menus, soothe your hurts, satisfy your most exotic tastes, offer a repast, special deliver forgotten purchases and patch up goofs with posies or confection. Russell Lund opened the world's first self-service supermarket on Lake Street in 1939. The family owned business has expanded to cover the metro area with a deluxe inventory of standard and hard-to-get grocery items. Foods from around the world tantalize palates of all kinds and present a resplendent agony of choice. Choose from 50 varieties of coffees, 30 different mustards, and if you can't find your specialty, fill out a request card and Lunds will deliver the goods. The <u>New York Times</u> or the <u>Wall Street Journal</u>, flowers in and out-of-season and spring waters of every stripe make a trip to Lunds a luxuriant excursion. Their unique refund policy is the ultimate boon of their devotion to the consumer.

Cossetta
211 West 7th Street
St. Paul 55102
222-3476

Mario Lanza's booming tenor and the aroma of calabria fill the air. Cheeses in huge wheels, garlics by the barrel and pizza by the slice have made Cossetta the premier Italian deli in the metro area. Cossetta has had several homes in St. Paul since opening as a fruit stand 80 years ago. It has maintained the culture of its Italian founders and today serves a diverse set of patrons who are simply interested in good food. Pastas in varieties that defy the imagination and gallons of olive oil as well as such menu items as mostaccioli and rotelle de mare bring the heritage of Italy and the flavor of another time to St. Paul.

El Burrito Marquet
200 Concord Street
St. Paul 55107
227-2192

The tastes are magnificent, the company is friendly and the heritage is treasured at El Burrito Marquet. Homemade Mexican pastries, tamales, burritos, chile, masa harina and chorizo make this Mexican grocery, bakery and deli a familiar spot for the Mexican-American community. But this spicy, full-flavored cuisine transcends nationality and El Burrito Marquet is a generally popular place on the west side of St. Paul. Pinatas and Mexican art decorate El Burrito and are available for sale.

Ingebretsen's Scandinavian Center
1601 East Lake Street
Minneapolis 55407
729-9333 gifts   729-9331 foods

During the holidays the lines of Scandinavians and neo-Scandinavians seeking lutefisk, goat cheese, fish pudding, lingonberry sauces, sandbakkels and lefse extend around the block. Since 1921, Ingebretsen's has been in the business of keeping Minnesotans of Scandinavian descent in touch with their heritage. The cheeses, sausages and other delicacies from Sweden, Denmark and Norway are a valued tradition for many area residents. Folk art and handicrafts make Ingebretsen's an excellent source of gifts and home decorative items. They carry porcelain and crystal, cookware and candle holders, books and records, needlework and knitting. They help Scandinavian-Americans discover and appreciate their roots.

Milano's
701 West Lake Street
Minneapolis 55408
827-1488

Authentic Mediterranean food and groceries including Greek and Mediterranean salads, hummos, tabouli salad, pastries and pita bread, marinated beef and lamb, Shaoka, linguine, primavera and Mediterranean potatoes are a sampling of the foods available at Milano's. This restaurant and deli has the intense flavors and pungent aromas of the Mediterranean in an inviting setting.

FARMERS' MARKETS
General Information: 227-8101
Hotline: 227-6856

Seasonal marketplaces for fresh garden produce. With the influx of Hmong immigrants who have settled in the Twin Cities, kan kon and bok choy have joined squash blossoms, patty pan, zucchini and a gorgeous selection of flowers. Whether a gourmand or a common garden variety cook, a Farmers' Market is a great place to spend an early morning. Call ahead for current crop information and various location schedules from April to November.

MINNEAPOLIS
> Central
> Lyndale and Glenwood
> Monday through Sunday
> 6:00 a.m. - 1:00 p.m.
>
> Nicollet Mall
> 4th Street through 10th Street
> Thursdays
> 6:00 a.m. - 6:00 p.m.

ST. PAUL
> Lowertown
> 290 East 5th Street (at Wall Street)
> Saturdays - 6:00 a.m. - 1:00 p.m.
> Sundays - 8:00 a.m. - 1:00 p.m.
>
> 7th Place Mall Market
> 7th and Wabasha Streets
> Thursdays - 10:00 a.m. - noon

* * * * * * * * *

The Lincoln Del
494 & France Avenue
Bloomington 55437
831-0780

4100 Minnetonka Boulevard
St. Louis Park 55416
927-9738

Even New Yorkers envy this one. Among the oldest and most respected delicatessens in the metro, The Lincoln Del has been pleasing generations of diners who seek rich, authentic kosher foods. Chopped or sauteed chicken livers and Reuben Sandwiches, blintzes, motza ball and other hearty soups, petit fours, European breads and a complete menu of American foods all boast of generous, robust flavor. Their pastry selection is heavy with layered and spiraling artistry. Both frozen specialties or ready-to-eat take-out are available. The Bloomington location has a full bar.

* * * * * * * * *

Fiori
17 N.E. 5th Street
Minneapolis 55413
623-1153

You're greeted by a pair of beautiful friendly Borzoi upon entering this exquisite hideaway full of fresh and dried flowers, wreaths, vines, topiary, French wire ribbon and ceramic pieces. A shop that is reminiscent of small French boutiques, Fiori creates plush and vivid romantic floral displays. A fabulous place.

Bachman's
6010 Lyndale Avenue South
Minneapolis 55419
861-7600 General Information
861-7311 Telephone Orders

Bachman's main store is garden, forest and festival. A tour of this floral center is visually and aesthetically stimulating. Their stock of flowers, trees and shrubs is unparalleled in its size, splendor and specialty. Cut flowers and plants for gifts or for the home, home landscaping, gardening tools and expert consultation for gardeners has made Bachman's a leader in the industry for 90 years. They believe that humans need plant life to be complete and happy. They fill this need 12 beautiful months a year. In addition to plants and trees, they have an excellent selection of planters, china, porcelains and Christmas decorations. Bachman's has a reputation for fast delivery to metro area homes and hospitals from any of their 29 stores.

Dundee Nursery
16800 Highway 55
Plymouth 55446
559-4016

There is common garden variety and everything else that grows at Dundee Nursery. Over 500 different varieties of perennials are available in the spring along with interesting and unusual trees, bushes and shrubs. They have a full floral service and lovely planters, benches and garden statuary.

Lyndale Garden Center
6412 Lyndale Avenue South
Richfield 55423
861-2221

Lyndale Garden Center has helped Minneapolis become one of the prettiest metropolitan areas in the country. Just about every flower or plant that will survive in Minnesota is found here. They also furnish expert advise and warm encouragement to customers at their Richfield and Burnsville stores.

Otten Brothers Nursery
2265 West Wayzata Boulevard
Long Lake 55356
473-5425

Otten's equips the western suburbs with quality nursery stock and professional landscape services. Each spring their supply of colorful and healthy bedding plants attracts thousands of customers eager to dress up their yards and patios. They have an excellent selection of shrubs and larger trees.

Wagner Greenhouse
6024 Penn Avenue South
Minneapolis 55419
922-6901

Wagner's call themselves "a growing tradition since 1901" and they certainly fill the bill. This greenhouse abounds with floral splendor. Opulent hanging baskets, packs of annuals and perennials, geraniums enough to light the city with color and tomato plants that will reap an abundant harvest make Wagner's one of the area's top-notch nurseries. Their annual Poinsettia Boutique, featuring over 40 exhibitors, is a breathtaking initiation into the holiday season.

Minnesota Landscape Arboretum
3675 Arboretum Road
Chanhassen 55317
443-2460

The Arboretum is feast of nature. This is a place to learn about the plant world and to experience it in great variety. On 950 acres of rolling hills, native woods and prairies and formal gardens, visitors can experience the rich beauty of nature year-round. The Linden Tree Gift Shop has gifts and domestics with botanical themes.

Bookdales
406 West 65th Street
Richfield 55423
861-3303

Book collectors and bibliophiles have a heyday at Bookdales. David Dale, a former newspaper editor, and his wife Joyce have a sense of things literary that is displayed in their fine collection of new and used books. Whether you want to buy or sell, you will be impressed by the depth and integrity of this book operation. They know the business and have made real connections with the book trade and its people.

Half Price Books
5011 Excelsior Boulevard
St. Louis Park 55416
922-2414

Half Price Books buys and sells used books, tapes, CD's and videos. The excellent, constantly updated inventory allows for hours of browsing. A vast majority of the stock is priced at half the original price or less. Remember, they also buy anything printed or recorded. Also St. Paul (699-1391) and Maplewood (773-0631).

Odegard Books
7505 France Avenue South
Edina 55435
831-9305

This elegant and spacious environment encourages curious minds and interested people to find their fortune in the world of books. Odegard has great depth in every category from the classics to best sellers to reference and special interest. At Odegard's books are a value to be cherished for a lifetime -- the completeness and the variety of their offerings say so.

Once Upon A Crime
604 West 26th Street
Minneapolis 55405
870-3785

This shop is a forum for fans of the suspense and mystery genre. They definitely have a specialized appeal and they do an extraordinary job of supplying sleuths, detectives and thrill seekers with the whole spectrum of suspense and mystery from Agatha Christie to Sara Paretsky.

Uncle Hugo's Science Fiction Bookstore
2864 Chicago Avenue South
Minneapolis 55407
824-6347

The largest science fiction specialty store on the planet. Earth to Uncle Hugo! The wacky and the wonderful frequent this enclave of the otherworldly. The atmosphere and the literature are made for lovers of aliens and the abstract universe. The superhuman, subhuman and extrahuman live happily here and share a building with Uncle Edgar's, which houses an enormous collection of mystery books. The combination of the two is too weird for words and somehow appeals to the fantasy in us all.

Applause
2841 Hennepin Avenue
Minneapolis 55408
871-9388

Open until midnight 365 days a year, Applause appeals to the music specialist and CD aficionada. With the most complete collection of classical music around, they are also up-to-date in pop, rock, funk and new age. Their sales personnel know what they're talking about and encourage informed buying. Minnesota Public Radio members get a 20% discount on classical recordings. Applause continually gets a standing ovation from sophisticated consumers of music. They also have shops in Ridgehaven Mall (591-0909) and on Snelling Avenue in St. Paul (644-8981).

The Electric Fetus
2010 - 4th Avenue South
Minneapolis   55404
870-9300

Music buffs of every persuasion will strike a chord at The Electric Fetus, consistently voted "Best Record Store" in the Twin Cities. The collection includes the latest pop sounds, but they are famous for unusual and little-known rock, jazz, and rhythm and blues recordings. Obscure artists and record companies can be found here as well as imports from Europe, Australia and Japan. The staff are experts in the trade. They believe in music and share their upbeat attitude with customers.

Homestead Pickin' Parlor
6625 Penn Avenue South
Richfield   55423
861-3308

Folk musicians have a guardian angel at Homestead Pickin' Parlor. They claim to be "Minnesota's only folk music store." Instruments, repairs, accessories, lessons and jam sessions as well as an excellent selection of recorded folk, bluegrass, blues, cajun, old time country and British Isles folk music on LP, cassette, and CD. They feature a large selection of children's recordings as well.

Musicland
705 Hennepin Avenue South
Minneapolis 55403
333-5611

The company that brought music to America's homes remains one of the giants of the industry. Musicland and Sam Goody stores are almost household words throughout the country by virtue of their ambitious merchandising effort and massive market presence. It is big in the metro area with 18 locations that always have what's hot in CD's, cassettes, videos and accessories. Musicland knows the market and continues to supply people of all ages what they want to hear. They will special order some 100,000 hard-to-find recordings.

Century Studios
200 - 3rd Avenue North
Minneapolis 55401
339-0239

High class stained glass! Beautiful Tiffany reproduction table and floor lamps are done in perfect detail. This stained glass studio will gladly produce custom orders and fill the most eccentric wishes. The time and labor required to create these masterpieces causes the prices to be high end. You own a genuine treasure when its yours.

Joe Diethelm
Josef's Art Glass
1213 West 24th Street
Minneapolis 55405
374-5848

Joe is one of a very few midwest artists actually staining glass. Joe does restoration and contemporary original works, but does not specialize in any one style. He is a careful student of many genres. Joe's work may be seen on St. Paul's Summit Avenue and Mt. Curve in Minneapolis, and is pictured in Architecture Minnesota. He is an intelligent and entertaining, hard-working, reliable gentleman whose creative works will enhance your decorating. Please call Joe for an appointment.

Gaytee Stained Glass, Inc.
2744 Lyndale Avenue South
Minneapolis 55408
872-4550

Gaytee has beautified Minneapolis since 1918 in a studio/warehouse where stained glass windows, doors and lamps are designed and built. Stained glass repair and restoration as well as retail supplies are available. Gaytee teaches their craft through a series of classes and are eager to share their affection for glass with the city.

Energy
Ridge Square North
13007 Ridgedale Drive
Minnetonka 55343
591-1040

Exhaustion in fashion. No size, no sport, no activity is out of style at Energy, the exercise clothing store. Prints and solids from small to XL, Tall and 1X through 4X will sustain you through the tough discipline of being fit and fashionable. If it isn't on the rack, Energy will custom make exercise gear for men, women and children. Leotards, thong leotards, warm-ups, leggings, tights, swimwear, sports bras to size 40DD, and tops represent over thirty top-name brands, including Baryshnikov body suits -- they have the right energy for you! Discounts are given to aerobic and dance instructors and to groups as well (cheerleading, dance, etc.)

Hoigaard's
36th St. exit at South Highway 100
St. Louis Park 55416
929-1351

For the Aspen set or for a night at Buck Hill, Hoigaard's has upheld an almost 100 year record of supplying rugged and elegant sporting goods. Their selection of indoor and outdoor casual furniture is good. Also St. Paul (484-8555).

Steve Hoag's Marathon Sports
2304 West 50th Street
Minneapolis 55410
920-2606

In the long run, this shop will serve you very well. Running suits, swimwear, mountaineering and biking gear are featured. Sales personnel will spend time with customers to help assure the right fit for the activity. Brands include Nike, Moving Comfort and Asics.

Bubbles & Scents
102 West 5th Street
Chaska 55318
448-6900
Please call The Connection (922-9000) for directions.

You can't go wrong. Scents and fragrances in all forms appear at immense savings at this open-to-the-public warehouse. The line of name brand fragrances includes potpourri, scented candles and sachets. Bath products include gelee, body lotions, hand soaps and powders. For children there are shampoos and bubble baths. Wicker baskets are available and can be transformed into gift-filled presentations for a nominal fee. Also Shakopee (496-4711).

Hudson Map Company
2510 Nicollet Avenue
Minneapolis 55404
872-8818

During 100 years in business, Hudson has become one of the country's premier map distributors. Their Twin Cities map book is the most authoritative guide to the area. Hudson has Cleartype and Rand McNally maps of all kinds -- wall, geological, survey, fishing, city, street, canoe trip and country. They also do precision work in enlarging, reproducing, framing and mounting services and they handle all map accessories.

Litin Paper Company
701 Washington Avenue North
Minneapolis 55401
333-4331

The first of its kind remains the best of its kind in discount paper products. Everything from paper cups, paper plates, paper clips, balloons, streamers and banners are in huge quantities. Seasonal decorating items are practical and imaginative. A visit to Litin offers the most economical way to dress up an occasion or affair.

Calamity Jeanne's
2460 West Industrial Boulevard
Long Lake 55356
473-0546

If Annie Oakley had shopped here Buffalo Bill wouldn't have had a chance! This is killer country and riding couture. Jeanne's ads offer "everything for horse and rider." She stocks Marlborough and Bond English boots, Texas, Acme, Dan Post and Justin western boots, saddles and horse equipment for English and western, hunt paraphernalia too. For men, women and kids, Calamity Jeanne's has the answer.

Schatzlein Saddle Shop
413 West Lake Street
Minneapolis 55408
825-2459

This family owned shop is the local headquarters for the horsey look. Western and English saddles, tack and square dance goods, boots by Dan Post, Acme and Dingo, sport coats by Pendleton and Circle S are some of the top value Western wear and gear at Schatzlein's. Their ladies' alligator boots are high fashion in any circle. In the business since 1907, Schatzlein can convert any dandy into a dude.

Hold It!
Centennial Lakes Plaza
7531 France Ave.
835-3010

A place for everything and everything in its place! In its three locations, Hold It! will help you organize and simplify your life. Lucite towel holders, tool caddies, hooks, hangers, laundry bags, desk organizers, gadgets and gimmicks to put it all together. Gain the organizational advantage with Hold It! Reasonably priced, well designed merchandise. Other locations: Minnetonka (544-5004) and St. Paul (635-0114)

Wicker Works
3054 Excelsior Boulevard
Minneapolis 55416
922-3032

Only God can make a tree, but oh what imagination can do to wood! Creative furniture design in pine, hickory, wicker, rattan, and twig makes for cozy and comfortable living. Accenting the furniture are beautiful fabrics in chintz and florals, tons of magnificent Ralph Lauren patterns and Beacon blankets in American Indian motifs. Distinctive style and true colors make Wicker Works a place where you can create your own special look. Periodic sales at unheard-of savings are an attraction here.

Plastic Bag Mart
511 Excelsior Boulevard East
Hopkins 55343
933-2366

"Just one word of advice, Ben. Plastics." The guy in "The Graduate" was right! There's a whole world of opportunity and convenience in plastic. The Plastic Bag Mart is a gold mine for those seeking any kind of plastic bags or essentials such as toilet tissue, paper towels, facial tissue, napkins and cups at low prices if purchased in quantity. They will deliver orders over $50 in the metro area and will custom make bags for your special needs. An example of the great deals is a box of 2-ply, 100 per box facial tissues for less than 50 cents per box when purchased in a case of 30.

Two's Company
4601 Bryant Avenue South
Minneapolis 55409
827-5396

Mother and daughter, Eleanor Mady and Sandy Mangel, offer a dazzling menagerie of china, glassware, crystal, porcelain, jewelry and soft goods straight from the snazziest East and West coast markets. There is a constant sense of spring and promise in this converted gas station. Their pillows, linens, dolls, picture frames, furniture, brass and wall decor will do more than spruce up your home; they'll brighten your whole life. Even if you're not in the mood to buy, a visit to Two's Company will lift the spirits and chase the blues away. It's therapeutic! Their stock of Limoges draws the most avid collectors.

Judith McGrann & Friends
3018 West 50th Street
Minneapolis 55410
922-2971

Head here if you're feeling or thinking tropical! Hand painted colorful T-shirts by Silent Fish, handcrafted furniture, topiaries by Tiny Trees with live ivies, rosemary and thyme, quilts, garden books, Japanese, Spanish and Turkish style books, "techno-romantic" jewelry by Thomas Mann featuring a variety of hearts, and a hilarious collection of note cards by Gallery Five, Design Design and Paper Sharks together with a large array of cat cards. The headquarters of whimsy.

Old America Store
4350 Xylon Avenue North
New Hope 55428
537-0585

This predominantly craft-oriented store is bulging with dried and silk flowers, baskets and frames, but its claim to fame is a huge inventory of Oriental blue and white porcelain at astoundingly low prices. Large, handpainted porcelain "fish bowls" inspired by those used to preserve pond carp during winter months in the Orient (and sell for hundreds at design studios) are a steal at Old America. They can be used as planters or as a table base.

Mill End Textiles
Eden Prairie (941-5350)
Crystal (533-6768)
Fridley (572-8449)
St. Paul-Sibley (698-7361)
St. Paul-Phalen (776-3099)

Reminiscent of the fabric warehouses in New York's fashion district, Mill End Textiles is piled to the ceiling with every imaginable pattern, texture, motif. Velours, denims, flannels, velvets, wools, sweatshirt prints, vinyls, bridal satins, terry toweling, stretch terry, corduroys, chamois, and kids patterns galore. Mill End is low in overhead, high in value. Sewing notions and accessories such as pillow forms, elastics, ribbons, velcro and hood strings make Mill End a dependable one-stop fabric shop.

The General Store of Minnetonka
14401 Highway 7
Minnetonka 55345
935-2215

The lore of the good old days is expressed in the handcrafted work at The General Store. Their endless variety of quality goods is made with a labor of love and carries a message of good feeling. In a rustic, multi-level setting, there is country, Americana, Minnesota artifacts, seasonal gifts and decorations, kitchen ware, personalized items, quilts, sweatshirts and old-fashioned candies. There are a zillion inexpensive favors for kids - erasers, pinwheels, stickers. The huge variety of merchandise at The General Store includes something from everyone's past.

Planes of Fame
N.W. Corner Flying Cloud Field
Eden Prairie 55344
941-2633

The history of World War II era aviation is on display at Planes of Fame. Twenty planes, memorabilia, displays and videos are housed in this 50,000 square foot museum. Guided tours and air rides are available. Videos bring to life the planes and the pilots from this exciting historical era. In the gift shop you will find books, models, sweaters, T-shirts and flight jackets. They have assembled a rich and authentic collection of valuable and interesting history.

Hagen's Furniture and Antiques
Valley Ridge Shopping Center
2021 West Burnsville Parkway
Burnsville 55337
894-5500
890-5221

This shop flows with an enormous inventory of new and used furniture. There is always a choice selection of fine dining and bedroom sets including major Chippendale and Queen Anne pieces. They accept furniture on consignment and do refinishing and restoration.

SERVICES

FURNITURE REPAIR

Anthony's Furniture Restoration
4553 Bryant Avenue South
Minneapolis 55409
824-1717

Tony Scahill and staff get their kicks restoring and repairing older furniture. They offer finish removal, refinishing, French polishing, restoration, repair, caning and upholstery services. They carry a large selection of appropriate fabrics. Business has been so good that Tony has opened a second shop (822-9050). Need we say more?

CANING

John Fox Chair Caning
722-8684

In today's technological world chair caners are rare. John Fox treats each piece like a precious object and weaves each stem delicately and exactly. He creates primitive luxury in cane. John works equally well with pressed-in cane or hand-woven cane.

CHINA, CRYSTAL and SILVER

Invisible China Repair and Restoration
8060 West First Lake Road
Willow River 55795
218/372-3120

A shattered dish, a cracked vase or a missing finger on a valued figurine need not be cause for despair. There is a solution to these unfortunate household accidents. Invisible China Repair and Restoration does exactly what it claims. Sue Sloper and Gerry Erickson apply skilled technique and loving care to each piece that comes to their shop. They have restored a Ming dynasty vase and Hummel figures that were victims of the 1988 San Francisco earthquake. You will feel comfortable leaving your treasured possessions with Sue and Gerry. Their artistry is expert and their craftsmanship impeccable.

China and Crystal Replacements
5613 Manitou Road
Excelsior 55331
474-6418

Do you need pieces to complete a family china service or have your tastes changed and you want to start over? It's all possible at China and Crystal Replacements, Inc. Out of stock and hard to find patterns on are available. They take custom and import orders and will buy your discontinued pattern outright or accept it on trade. Whether you need a current pattern at a super price or a discontinued pattern, this is the place to go.

Mr. & Mrs. Chips
Donald & Elsie Weiss
Route 2, Box 34A
Brandon 56315
1-524-2602

Don't throw away your chipped or broken glassware. The most scrutinizing critic will be hard pressed to find the crack in your china or the chip in your crystal after a trip to Mr. & Mrs. Chips! They can only be found at antique shows. Call to see when and where you can take advantage of their excellent work.

Gerald Ludwig Art Work Repair
2721 June Avenue North
Golden Valley
522-9376

Your family heirlooms and personal art and antique collections are worth the best treatment. Gerald Ludwig restores glass, china, crystal, statuary, pottery and carvings. Preserve their beauty and value. Ludwig does flawless and indetectable work.

Oexning Silversmiths
9 North 4th Street
Minneapolis 55401
332-6857

It's almost like magic. Regardless of how badly damaged a silver piece may be, Oexning Silversmiths give it new life and restore it to its original beauty. They do plating, refinishing, replacing, straightening, polishing, lacquering and oxidizing. Whatever your needs -- coffee sets, trays, flatware, musical instruments or church accessories, Oexning can save an heirloom from the past or create one for the future.

CLOCK REPAIR

Valley Clockworks
7958 Highway 55
Golden Valley
544-8046

Tucked away on the northwest corner of Highway 55 and Winnetka is the Twin Cities' master clock repair center. Owner Bob Ockenden has been fixing clocks, watches and jewelry for 23 years and is dedicated to high grade work and personalized service. If you're looking for a special grandfather clock or a French 18th Century clock, let Bob know and he'll be happy to locate it for you. Every inch of this tiny space is covered with clocks of all types -- old and new -- all available for purchase. Bob makes house calls if your masterpiece is not easily transported.

DRAPERY AND CARPET CLEANING

Darling Drapery and Carpet Cleaning
4805 Nicollet Avenue
Minneapolis 55409
827-5461

Call them if you need to hear a friendly voice. They answer, "Hello Darling." This family owned and operated business has provided top quality cleaning for Twin Cities draperies and carpets since 1922. They offer free pickup and delivery and cash and carry service for rugs, carpets, draperies, comforters, bedspreads, upholstery and other fabric household items. They do have minimum charges for full-service, but often offer specials in the daily newspapers.

CUSTOM DRAPERIES/BEDDING

Mary Elizabeth Draperies
479-1951

Mary Elizabeth is the Wonder Woman of the sewing trade! She can make draperies, valances, swags, Roman shades, bedspreads, dust ruffles, canopies and duettes. Her work is exceptional and very reasonably priced. Hundreds of sample books from which fabrics may be chosen are available.

Aero Custom Window Fashions
860-6393

For over 45 years, Aero Custom Window Fashions has offered its customers both the convenience of shopping at home and the choice of more than 5,000 fabrics. Aero can meet all your window treatment needs: custom draperies, top treatments, vertical blinds, mini blinds, pleated shades and shutters. Aero also offers custom bedspreads so that you can create a complete bedroom ensemble. All Aero work is backed by an unconditional "Perfection Guarantee", assuring that the fashions ordered will be measured, manufactured and installed to the window's exact specifications.

Based in Minnesota, Aero has stores in several parts of the county, including two in the Twin Cities area (in Roseville and Burnsville). Perfect window fashions are just a phone call away. To schedule a no-cost, no-obligation Shop-At-Home appointment, call the above number in the Twin Cities or 1-800-788-AERO anywhere in Minnesota.

INVISIBLE WEAVING

Wizard Weavers
12 South 6th Street - Room 257
338-6413

Valued and valuable clothing need not be discarded or patched. There is indeed wizardry in the way Levera Bacon is able to rehabilitate a torn or worn garment. Wizard reweaves damaged clothing to original condition. Sweaters, wool jackets and pants, blankets and tablecloths and just about any fabric that needs mending can find a friend at the Wizard Weavers.

BOOKS

Arch Books
Minneapolis
927-0298

The books we read in childhood remain with us forever. Over 35,000 titles of out-of-print children's and illustrated books are in stock at Arch Books. Revisit old friends like <u>Heidi</u> and <u>The Red Pony</u> by contacting Arch Books by phone. The entire inventory is computerized for efficiency. If your title is not in stock, they will do a title search.

BUTTONS

Minnesota State Button Society
Contact: Lib Welshons
1-565-2340

Do you want to dress up an ordinary frock or upgrade a bargain basement special? With the right buttons you can perform magic. The Twin Cities lacks a retail outlet devoted to the art of buttonry. The Minnesota State Button Society is dedicated to the study of the history of buttons. At monthly meetings they share knowledge and experiences. Society members are able to assist you in locating the perfect button.

LAMPS & SHADES

Michael's Lamp Studio
3101 West 50th Street
Minneapolis 55410
926-9147

Do you have a great lamp in storage because you don't know where to find the perfect shade or where to have it rewired or repaired? Michael's has one of the largest selections of lampshades in the Twin Cities. Always take the lamp needing a shade to the shop because Michael cautions, "Choosing a shade without the lamp is like buying a hat without your head."

Anderson's Lampshades
263 West 7th Street
St. Paul 55102
222-6131

Anderson's will search the world over looking for the shade, finial, parts or particulars your lamps need. This is the Twin Cities largest lampshade store with thousands to choose from. The number and variety will dazzle you and your purchase will fit exactly your personal tastes. View the spectacular world of lampshades at Anderson's.

RENTALS

Apres, Inc.
9057 Lyndale Avenue South
Bloomington 55420
881-3991

You'll be the talk of the party crowd whether it's an intimate evening for two or a grand soiree. After visiting their showroom, Apres will execute your ideas for spectacular entertaining. Chairs and tables, coat racks, bars, dance floors, tents and canopies, fans, heaters, generators, hot dog and popcorn machines, lawn games and volleyball sets, and, of course, china, flatware, glassware, beverage fountains and a complete line of disposables. All the trappings to dazzle your guests and enhance your reputation as a host are on display at this first class establishment. For occasions to remember, Apres, Inc. has the answer.

CLEANING

Dale Services
2005 Shaughnessy Circle
Long Lake 55356
473-7094

Revive your household with expert and experienced hands. The most laborious parts of household maintenance, i.e., carpets, upholstery, floors -- even house washing -- are done by trained, trustworthy, security-conscious pros. And...yes, they _do_ do windows!

TYPEWRITER REPAIR

Vale Typewriter Repair
6319 Penn Avenue South
Richfield 55423
869-3664 or 866-2513

An honest-to-goodness repair service that is speedy, courteous and efficient. Vale repairs typewriters, adding machines and computer printers. They have the know-how of IBM and the service of the shop on Main Street. Vale also sells new and used typewriters, word processors and adding machines. If you have older office equipment that needs repair, don't despair. Vale has the experience and parts to keep the office, at home or at your place of business, in production.

PHOTOGRAPHERS

Amundson and McDonald Photography
205 N. River Street
Delano 55328
1-972-6631

Painstaking detail, artistic flourish and photographic integrity make Amundson and McDonald one of the area's best photographers. From fashion shots to commercial layouts, from landscapes to family events and portraits, Amundson and McDonald has established a reputation for capturing the personality and spirit of their subjects. Check out the back cover of this book!

Daniels Animal Portraits
908 Mainstreet
Hopkins 55343
935-4493

It may be a sign of a society that has too much, but photographer Ken Ahlstrom is doing to dogs what Ansel Adams did to trees, capturing their natural and essential images. Ahlstrom is a four-time winner of the Minnesota Sweepstakes Award for overall photographic excellence as well as the winner of regional and national awards. In 1981 he combined his love for animals with his profession and has since photographed more than 1,000 dogs. He is known in the industry as the "Canine King" but captures cats and other animals with equal skill.

Leonard Dixon
Gallery West Photography
14119 Holly Road
Eden Prairie 55346
937-8235

Wedding and bridal specialists. Naturalness is the most telling feature of a Gallery West work.

Gianneti Photography
Joe Gianneti
119 North 4th Street
Minneapolis 55401
339-3172

The photograph as art piece is the type of work produced by Joe Gianneti. He does business and commercial photography. He has done work for the Children's Theatre and the Guthrie, models, newspaper pieces, business and trade brochures and annual reports. Gianneti's work is an influence throughout Minneapolis.

Barbara Lund Photography
925-5194

National award-winning photographer Barbara Lund will capture the essence of your family in an environmental portrait. Executive portraiture is a specialty as well. Barbara "has camera, will travel." She could make you famous!

BY APPOINTMENT ONLY

Bravo Bras
511 - 11th Avenue South
Minneapolis 55415
338-3353

Bravo Bras caters to the special needs of women. This by-appointment-only store helps women requiring mastectomy or reduction bras, breast prostheses or a custom fit. Owner Judy Anderson brings a nursing background and 23 years of fitting consultation to this shop which offers assistance to ladies of all shapes and sizes. Lingerie -- including long waltz length gowns, pajamas, lace tights and body suits, teddys and camis -- is available in sizes small to 4X. Swimwear is available to size 52 and queen size hosiery is stocked. You will feel better about who you are and how you look with the correct fit from Bravo Bras.

D. Dawley & Co.
10740 Lyndale Avenue South
Suite 20
Minneapolis 55420
885-0053

Complete your ensemble with a deliciously spectacular hat! Dolores Dawley and her 15 representatives in the Twin Cities, Rochester and Phoenix put together fantastically fun shows in private homes, at country clubs, for women's groups, university or fashion gatherings. They shop the world's hat markets from South America and San Francisco to Prague, for hats and headpieces for men, women and children. Visit the showroom featuring 3,000 fabulous hats!

The Carlisle Collection, LTD.
Jan Lee
2570 Cedar Ridge Road
Wayzata 55391
475-2531

Four times a year Jan Lee presents in her home a collection of traditional, high quality suits, dresses and sportswear which are shown by appointment. Fine fabrics, gathered by Carlisle's designers from the world's most prestigious fabric houses, are selected to maximize wardrobe possibilities. This is home shopping at its finest with expertise offered in coordinating and fitting. Jan will assist you in selecting what best suits your needs.

Doncaster
Gai Skramstad
28020 Woodside Road
Excelsior 55331
474-5374

Doncaster presents unique, yet classic styling, dynamic color and pattern selection and rich fabrics in their direct sale of women's fashions. Sales consultants invite clients to their homes or an outside showroom to view the ready-made collection or to create a custom-cut ensemble. Doncaster is known for impeccable tailoring, generous seams and hems, and hand-finishing on all garments. Doncaster fashions are sold as coordinated separates which allow clients to match or complement other separates in the collection. For those who wish to invest in their wardrobe, Doncaster has wonderful creations. Sizes range from 4 petite to 20W.

Big Kids, Inc.
4816 Excelsior Boulevard
St. Louis Park 55416
920-4588

This is having it all. A salon committed to giving customers a glowing appearance from head to toe based in the latest concepts in hair cutting, styling and chemical artistry. Their goal at Big Kids is not just the finished product, although the look will be great. Their stylists educate and train customers to be involved in their own health and appearance. Hair styling, facials, waxing, manicures, pedicures, full-body treatments are part of their comprehensive approach to personal care. Is it luxury or good sense? Make a date with owner Ron Peterson for a superb haircut and some supreme schmoozing!!.

Bellezza
Deephaven Court
18279 Minnetonka Boulevard
Deephaven 55391
449-8823

In Italian bellezza means "beautiful and balanced." That expression is transformed into a skin and body care concept that is healthy for the mind and the body. European facials, therapeutic massage, aromatherapy treatments, waxing, tinting and makeup are all done to give you a beautiful and balanced life. Bellezza's product lines include Paul Scerri from Switzerland, Yonka from France, Bindi from India, Sabar from Israel and Paul Herb from Minneapolis.

The Day Spa
3300 Edinborough Way
Edina 55435
830-0100

Life is too short not to indulge in its pleasures. The Day Spa will transport you for an hour or a day to some ethereal spot where cares and imperfections are forgotten. Their numerous services include three types of facials, massages, body wraps, manicures, pedicures and Janet Sartin make-up. A Metamorphosis Day costs $145.00, a Mini-Metamorphosis is $75.00. They have interesting and clever jewelry to accent the new you. A hair salon next door is terribly handy in your pursuit of Aphrodite or Adonis.

Estee Lauder Spa at Dayton's Southdale
924-6638

The prestige and the know-how of the internationally acclaimed Estee Lauder bring a ritual of pleasure and necessity. Your physical and emotional health will benefit from the spa's Day of Beauty (5-1/2 hours) which includes facial, massage, manicure, pedicure, hand and feet treatment and makeover. Take a trip all by yourself and return relaxed, refreshed and invigorated. La Dolce Vita!

The Marsh
15000 Minnetonka Boulevard
Minnetonka   55345
935-2202

You can hear the soothing sounds of rippling streams and feel the gentle breezes touch your face in the atmosphere of The Marsh. The Marsh is a spa for cardiovascular health. Everything is geared for aerobic exercise and wellness is touted stylishly. In the gift shop you will find jackets, sweats, streetwear, workout gear, warm-up and hosiery. Classes are open to the public by day, week or month. The pool is available for members only. The soups, salads and brownies in the restaurant are nutritionally correct and fabulously tasty.

Mary Kay Cosmetics
Alison Amy Stephens
Executive Senior Director
7101 Lanham Lane
Edina   55439
941-5737

Cast off that frumpy facade! Sonja Suburb or Ursula Urban -- whatever your style -- let the professionals do the primping for you. Beautiful, healthy skin is in! There is a unique glamour in every face which Mary Kay can enhance in you.

Victorian Treasures
12148 Madison Street N.E.
Blaine, MN 55434
755-6302

Lost elegance is found in Blaine -- of all places! Laurie Pekarik will custom design a garment especially for you, a child or a doll. She is a purveyor of high quality imported fabrics, exquisite imported laces, and Swiss embroideries. Laurie teaches French heirloom sewing, Battenberg lace, shadow embroidery, English smocking and tatting in her studio (by appointment) or she will travel to you.

STILLWATER
Zip Code 55082

The St. Croix River Valley is home to some of Minnesota's most beautiful scenery and most unique shopping opportunities. Foremost among the river towns is Stillwater where some 90 businesses are located. Stillwater was once the center of the lumber industry in the Northwest. It was the site, in 1848, of the Minnesota Territorial convention and was the first official town site in the state. The civic activism and entrepreneurial spirit of its early citizens made Stillwater a major force in the development of Minnesota. Stillwater thrives today as an inviting place to live and a prodigious shopping area. It is a picturesque city that has retained charming elements of the past while changing and progressing with time.

The business community in Stillwater is lively. Some of the most interesting antique stores, galleries and specialty shops in the region are found on its Main Street. Stillwater is very much a town where the old and the new are both cherished qualities. Vintage frocks and the latest fashions are equally available as well as home furnishings, gifts, sporting goods, medical, banking and legal services, restaurants and lodging. The unique and somewhat exclusive quality of the merchandise causes prices to be somewhat high.

You can <u>easily</u> spend a day doing Stillwater's shops and enjoying its beauty. We caution that walking is not easy here -- up and down hills, lots of stairs in many of the shops, so do what mother always told you: "Wear comfortable shoes!"

The Lowell Inn
102 North Second Street
439-1100

For almost half a century, the Lowell Inn has been receiving rave revues as one of the most distinguished inns in America. The Williamsburg theme is carried out in the decor of 25 guest rooms and three dining rooms, The George Washington, The Garden Room and The Matterhorn. This red brick retreat with a spacious veranda and majestic colonnades offers hotel accommodations in magnificently appointed rooms and suites.

Stillwater River Trolley
430-0352

The trolley will allow you to explore firsthand the corners and cul de sacs, the many hills and narrow streets of this historic city. The breathtaking view from the scenic bluffs overlooking the St. Croix Valley, stately homes and steepled churches -- all part of the folklore and history of Stillwater -- are in brilliant focus on this tour.

* * * * * * * * *

Andiamo Showboat
430-1236

Cruise the scenic and historic St. Croix River on this large, luxurious stern-wheeler. Enjoy fresh-water fish or prime rib while listening to the sounds of New Orleans jazz. Under the moonlight the full beauty of the river and the port of Stillwater can be truly appreciated.

* * * * * * * * *

ST. CROIX RIVER EXCHANGE
317 Main Street
Stillwater, MN 55082

The five shops in the St. Croix River Exchange range from **Fancy Nancy's** baubles to the beautiful yarns and threads at the **Busy Needle Stitchery**. The **Ball of Wax Candle Shop**, **Barbara Ann's Fudge Shop**, and the **Hmong Shop** make the Exchange a gift-buyers heaven.

Brick Alley Books
423 South Main Street
439-0266

If you browse, you'll buy at this store filled with enticing titles and fanciful greeting cards, colorful kites, festive pinatas and many types of music. Classical, children's, and New Age compact discs and tapes make the Brick Alley a stimulating store.

The Bird House, Inc.
5901 Omaha Avenue
439-1923

Wildbird watchers, ornithologists and just plain nice people will flock to this complete and unique bird store. A gourmet selection of bird seed and mixes, feeders and field guides for avid and casual enthusiasts are offered at the Bird House. Beyond the basics the Bird House has an imaginative selection of gifts ranging from elaborate wood inlaid pieces from India to refrigerator magnets from LaCrosse.

The Cottage In The Woods
114 North Main Street
439-3311

Its name and its merchandise conjures up images of gentle pastimes and quaint pleasures. A shop run by mother-daughter team Sharon and Kerilyn Stefan and friend Marianne McDaniel. The enchanting themes and effects make Cottage a great source of gifts and goodies. In the front window there's a wolf dressed to look like grandma tucked into bed. A white picket fence winds throughout the displays of willow furniture pieces, Waverly fabrics, bag lady or watermelon pillows. Cards, stationery, soaps and scents are carefully selected and imaginatively presented. Nestled along the wooded path and throughout the Cottage are Little Red Riding Hood baskets, each unique and personalized for any special occasion.

Main Street Antiques
118 North Main Street
430-3110

Great finds and minute treasures are everywhere at Main Street. Their specialty is kitchenalia including spice racks, salt & peppers, canisters, coffee pots, Tom & Jerry mugs, domed cake plates, enamelware, skillets, trays and sifters. Floor to ceiling, wall to wall, Main Street is jammed full.

OLD POST OFFICE SHOPS
220 East Myrtle Street
Stillwater, MN 55082

The stately old post office in Stillwater remains a gathering spot for visitors and tourists. Its prominent location in the downtown landscape invites visitors.

The Thatchentree
439-2996

Gund stuffed animals, Victorian jewelry and lovely laces are part of this collection of gifts and goodies.

Token Creek
430-1431

Their extensive collection of Running Press miniatures can occupy shoppers for hours! Both traditional and innovative gifts and decorative items such as sampler patterns, throws, plastic floral trays, silk and dried flowers, napkins and placemats by Caspari and scented candles are found here in colorful abundance.

Emery House
439-1771

There is everything new and upbeat here. An enormous selection of Pimpernel coasters, placemats and trays in endless designs, French wired ribbon, gourmet art (Get this! Peppers and onions floating in liquid in a glass rolling pin, mounted for wall display), elegant topiary trees, gorgeous Bita baskets from France. Their real blockbuster item is room dividers and screens in custom upholstered fabrics. Owner Susan Emery Roettger will consign fine antiques. She currently has a gorgeous Chickering & Sons piano dated 1857 and priced at $14,000. Merchandise of all kinds has a lovely home at Emery.

* * * * * * * * *

Tea & Company
439-1726

You will be enticed by the croissant sandwiches, salads, ice creams and the Margarita pie. Then you'll be fascinated by the profusion of tea pots, miniature tea sets and decorative stained glass pieces. This is a nice spot to take "time out".

* * * * * * * * *

Mulberry Point Antiques
270 North Main Street
430-3630

The goods of 65 dealers are beautifully displayed and presented on four floors. Major furniture pieces such as a rosewood and walnut Renaissance revival step-in dressing case (Circa 1870) and Victorian Eastlake ensembles are here. Accessories such as brown Staffordshire china, Belleek and Steuben. Novelties such as sardine can openers and bar pitchers can be spotted and collectibles such as baseball cards and thimbles. Mulberry has representation from all eras and is the classiest antique shop in town. You'll fall in love with wooden chairs and headboards hand painted with flowers by Afton artist Camie Erickson.

More Antiques
312 North Main Street
439-1110

There's a broad range of antiques here from a Johannes Derr, Pa. Kentucky Rifle dated 1818 ($4,750) to "Royal Vienna" handpainted coffee service from 1890 for $2,200. The supply of interesting and exquisite pieces is extraordinary. A special bonus: primitive and Scandinavian items.

J. Clark Clocks
113 South Main Street Square
430-2685

For those who have an interest in time pieces, J. Clark Clocks has a vast variety to choose from. They specialize in restoration of antique movements and cases. Inventory includes interesting mantel and wall clocks and pocketwatches of all ages.

ISAAC STAPLES SAWMILL

The 80 foot smokestack still stands as a memorial to milling in the St. Croix Valley. Located on the far end of the city of Stillwater, Isaac Staples Sawmill has an aura of yesterday. There hasn't been much change or updating since the Mill was built in 1853 so the combinations of the old and the new are very interesting. Five businesses are housed in the Mill.

The Mill Antiques
410 North Main Street
430-1816

Reopened recently after a major fire, there are reunited again over 60 antique dealers on three levels at the Mill. The collections represent the long and rich history of Minnesota sprinkled with American collectibles and odds and ends. From tools by the dozens to tins by the score, Mill Antiques has it all.

Crystal Magic Rock Shop
402 North Main Street
430-9180

Unique jewelry and gifts are handcrafted in this shop. You can carry the geology and history of Minnesota around with you in their customized jewelry.

Images of the Past
402 North Main Street
439-1252

Don't throw it away! The precious family photo that you thought was beyond repair can be beautifully restored and preserved. Images of the Past loves the challenge of bringing life back to old pictures. They remove scratches and stains, add missing parts, combine people from different photographs. They also sell acid-free albums that will protect your memories for future generations.

Northern Vinyards
402 North Main Street
430-1032

Owned and operated by the Minnesota Winegrowers Cooperative, wines at Northern Vinyards are made from grape varieties locally grown by members. The wines include varietals made from the French Hybrids Seyval, Foch and Millot and local blends including grapes such as Aurore, Canadice, Kay Gray, Edelweiss and St. Croix. Stop by for a taste or a bottle of home grown vintage.

Glasspectacle
402 North Main Street
439-0757

Magnificent glass pieces by Josh Simpson, a Corning Museum of Glass award winner. The highly collectible glass planets and mega worlds along with perfumes, paperweights, animals, exquisite vases, kaleidoscopes, stained glass shades and hangings make this place sparkle.

AFTON
Zip Code 55001

Visitors to this area in the mid-1880's were reminded of Robert Burn's poem, "Flow Gently, Sweet Afton" and thence came the city's name. Located on the banks of the St. Croix, just twenty miles from Stillwater, Afton is a city rich in history but with a progressive business climate that is very much in touch with the present. In the center of this quiet residential community is a small business district of restaurants, marinas, shops and services. Most of the village businesses are located in 19th Century houses or buildings which make a charming shopping experience.

The Historic Afton House Inn
436-8883

Built in 1867 and on the Historic Register, the Afton House offers fine dining and comfortable lodging in traditional ambiance. Its Catfish Saloon is open daily for hamburgers and sandwiches. There are twelve country rooms for overnight lodging.

The Afton Toy Shop
3290 St. Croix Trail South
436-1150

Not of the mass-market variety, the Afton Toy Shop has unusual and delightful goods for children of all ages. Hard to find Russian stacking dolls of Gorby, Lenin, Brezhnev, Stalin, and Khrushchev, fabulous costumes for kids and baby clothes are a part of this imaginative collection.

Baglio's
436-1506

Set in the original bank building, Baglio's features select designer fashions and accessories. Owners Lisa and Bill Baglio will proudly show you the bank's original safe and a 1914 stock certificate.

Original Paintings by Cami Erickson
369 Croix View Drive
436-7750

Ivy and roses, morning glories and fish. Painted furniture that transforms any room into a garden of color and texture. The subtle details and rich nuances of flowers can be woven into any motif or style. Ms. Erickson's work is simply wonderful and has found a perfect home in the Afton community.

Selma's Ice Cream Parlor
436-8067

More than just great ice cream. Homemade cones, custom created flavors, candies, specialties and novelties are offered. The ice cream parlor of the past exists here.

Squire House Gardens
3390 St. Croix Trail South
436-8080

Gardeners and flower lovers will go nuts at this place. Surrounded by everything floral from Botanic Garden china to garden tools and water wands, the world of flowers is prized at Squire House Gardens. Whimsical paintings on the walls and floors embellish the colorful and tasteful designs throughout this charming historic house.

THE HIAWATHA VALLEY

The scenic area along the Mississippi from Hastings to LaCrosse is known as the Hiawatha Valley. Towering cliffs and serene backwaters provide a view that rivals the world's greatest riverways in beauty and grandeur. The mighty Mississippi has given inspiration to the towns and villages along its shores. These communities are the site of shops, motels, restaurants, marinas and services which provide business and pleasure for thousands of visitors each year. The Hiawatha Valley offers a combination of natural beauty and commercial enterprise that makes it an attractive shopping and recreation area. A motor tour along the Great River Road will show an area of natural beauty and interesting history. Driving the Great River Road, visitors will see small towns each with its own characteristic charm. Interspersed among the towns are parks, scenic lookouts, historic forts and monuments. One of the most spectacular points along the river is the majestic Lake Pepin.

HASTINGS
Zip Code 55033

Located on the banks of the Mississippi, historic Hastings participated in the birth of Minnesota and today is an active partner in the contemporary life of the state. It is a tourist site, with recreational parks, boating, swimming and fishing. Its proximity to the metro area makes it a vital and lively place to live. It is the county seat of the progressive and rapidly growing Dakota County. The history of Hastings is very much entwined with the growth of the State of Minnesota. Hastings was a growing river town in the latter part of the 19th Century. Because of increasing river trade, improved transportation was needed. Out of this need, the city's most famous landmark was born. The idea of the famous Spiral Bridge was conceived and in 1895 it was opened for traffic. The unique design made the Spiral Bridge an engineering feat and an instant tourist attraction. The burden of traffic and the advent of the automobile placed too great a strain on the structure and in 1951, amid considerable protest, the Spiral Bridge was demolished. Hastings today is a major stopping point for travelers on the Mississippi between St. Paul and St. Louis. Lock and Dam No. 2 has been a popular tourist attraction for more than 50 years. The Hastings business community offers a wide variety of shopping experiences. There are great eateries, clothiers, gift and specialty shops, antique shops, interior design centers, gallery and framing shops, craft and pet stores, home improvement centers, health, beauty and fitness salons, legal and financial services.

Alexis Bailly Vineyard
18200 Kirby Avenue
437-1413

Perhaps the most unique enterprise in the Hastings business community is this small vineyard that produces excellent wine from wholly Minnesota grown grapes. Alexis Bailly has won 12 awards including three "best of class." The winery is open to the public from June to October for tours, samplings and sales.

Fancy That!
110 East Second Street
437-6851

Clever cards, gifts, candles, books and a permanent Christmas room. Old fashioned charm with a Victorian flair. Be sure to see the uncaged and flying collection of live birds in the window of the Tele-Systems Associates just two doors from Fancy That! Most entertaining.

RED WING
Zip Code 55066

An hour south of the Twin cities, at the head of beautiful Lake Pepin and nestled between limestone bluffs carved centuries ago by the Mississippi river, lies Red Wing -- one of southern Minnesota's most historic sites. The city's name came from an old Sioux chief "Wings of Scarlet", and Red Wing became the county seat of Goodhue County in 1854, four years before Minnesota became a state. The founders were people with entrepreneurial and civic ambitions who built a city that was advanced in planning and distinctive in style along the rough banks of the Mississippi.

Today Red Wing takes advantage of both the past and present and attracts year-round visitors. Shopping in Red Wing is plentiful -- from the city's two foremost products, Red Wing Pottery and Red Wing Boots -- to antiques. On summer days a replica of a San Francisco trolley car travels the streets and transports visitors to the historic Pottery District, adding to the stimulating atmosphere of this old port city.

Telephone numbers listed for Red Wing are area code 612 but require a 1 before the long distance number when calling from the Twin Cities. Some stores have metro lines or 800 numbers which are listed for your convenience.

St. James Hotel
406 Main Street
Metro Line: 227-1800
or 338-2846

The elegance of the Victorian Era and symbols of gracious, genteel living make the St. James one of the most popular and arresting hotels in the Midwest. Built as a testimony to Red Wing's prosperity, the St. James has been host to the ordinary and the famous for over a century. Nearly half of the 60 guest rooms have a view of the Mississippi River and the Red Wing bluffs. The St. James has a unique shopping court with eleven specialty stores. The St. James Hotel is a step back in time, a place to forget the 20th Century and enjoy a bit of ease and luxury.

Red Wing Pottery Sales, Inc.
1890 West Main Street
388-3562

One of the oldest and most respected names in pottery and stoneware, Red Wing Pottery Sales is headquarters for consistently good reductions on quality china. They handle over 400 patterns with discounts from five to twenty percent. The national reputation for excellence enjoyed by the name Red Wing lives today and guarantees customers quality merchandise and service. This company, part of Minnesota's proud history, offers a touch of the past and outstanding quality goods.

Loons and Ladyslippers
1890 West Main Street
388-3562
Toll Free 1-800-228-0174

Loons and Ladyslippers has zillions of items covered with images of the official state bird and flower. Great Minnesota memorabilia including wildlife art, decoys, Minnetonka moccasins, whimsical watercolors by local artist Jean Haefele stretch the imagination.

Pottery Salesroom

Outdoor jardinieres by the truckload, garden statuary, bird feeders and lawn accessories of every size and design. You can dress up your lawn and garden at good prices.

Wicks 'n' Sticks
388-1841

This outlet store offers everything imaginable in candles at the best prices. Stock up for every season of the year and for everyday at Wicks 'n' Sticks.

Winona Knits
Next to the Pottery
1902 West Main
388-5738

America's oldest and largest sweater retailer, Winona Knits presents a wide collection of sweater fashion for the whole family. They carry coordinated tops and bottoms and top-notch sweater care products. Their return policy adds to this company's reputation for quality and service.

Pottery Place
2000 West Main Street
388-1428

Pottery Place is one of Red Wing's foremost attractions. It is a unique shopping area in which the past and the present join in a busy and exciting market. The turn-of-the-century building reflects its history of pottery making while offering contemporary amenities and shopping opportunities for varied tastes and budgets. Displays of the original cast iron equipment and pottery molds, and the world famous Red Wing pottery logo, recall the history of one of Minnesota's most successful early industries. Visitors will linger a bit in the past as they walk the tiled and wooden pathways leading through a maze of shops and boutiques. Manufacturers' outlets at Pottery Place provide direct access to factory merchandise at discount prices. There are also retail stores, restaurants and antique shops at Pottery place.

Some of the outstanding outlets here include the following:

Aileen
388-8457

Aileen has ladies sportswear in petite, missy and plus sizes at 35 to 70% off retail value.

Bass Shoes
388-6967

One of the world's foremost shoe manufacturers carries children's, women's and men's shoes from dressy to casual. They also have excellent prices on socks, purses and leather and canvas accessories.

Benetton Factory Outlet
388-6967

Up to 70% savings on Benetton's colorful and dramatic sportswear for men and women.

Corning/Revere Factory Store
388-0701

Featuring a wide selection of Corning and Revereware products at substantial savings on overstock and discontinued items. They also have cosmetic seconds as well as a huge supply of coordinating accessories.

Van Heusen
388-0817

A true manufacturer's outlet store. Save 30 to 60% on Van Heusen dress and sportswear. Lady Van Heusen sportswear and designer brand names.

The Wallet Works
388-7031

This factory owned and operated store offers first quality leather wallets, clutches, key cases and accessories. You can save on name brand briefcases, luggage, handbags and travel gifts.

Winona Glove Sales
388-0101

A wonderful variety of dress and work gloves, purses, wallets, ski accessories, woolen caps and scarves, socks and moccasins.

The Woolen Mill
388-8857

The blankets that keep America warm are offered at attractive discounts. Men's and women's jackets and sweaters are also priced to sell.

Old Main Street Antiques
388-1371

You'll be amazed with what's old. There is a tremendous collection of reasonably priced antiques representing all eras and styles. Twenty plus dealers in this third floor shop will have something you can't resist.

Memories Antiques
388-6446

Their stock will invoke special feelings and fond memories of the people and places in your past. Ten dealers have a large selection of well selected and cared for merchandise.

Pottery Place Antiques
388-7765

Here are eight resourceful, relentless collectors of great old pieces who present their finds in this fascinating shop.

Ice House Antiques, Inc.
1811 West Main Street
388-8939

An old ice house becomes a two-story antique haunt crammed with quality French and English furniture, large vases, jewelry, china, country linens and quilts and children's furniture. This clean and classy shop is just down the road from the Pottery District.

Harry & Jewel's Victorian Antiques
1010 Hallstrom Drive
388-5989

Important furniture pieces and well-chosen accessories are the order at this lovely shop. Rosewood and walnut, marble topped pieces, exquisite clocks and vintage lamps make Harry & Jewel's one of the area's finest. Open by chance or appointment.

Teahouse Antiques
927 West Third Street
388-3669

Teahouse is located in the historic Octagon House, one of the city's most distinctive architectural structures. Built in 1857, the house is on the National Register of Historic Places and is open for tours by appointment. Teahouse Antiques is a tiny, two-room shop in the inner sanctum of Octagon House. A general line of antiques is offered with an assortment of unusual memorabilia.

The River Peddler
120 Bush Street
388-5990

Located in the lower level of the St. James Hotel, the River Peddler has wonderful pieces of furniture, lovely glassware and crystal, unique mirrors and interesting, unusual primitives. Merchandise is displayed in a bright, homey atmosphere.

Mickey Finn's Country Furnishings
207 Bush Street
388-0144

Right in the heart of downtown Red Wing, across the street from the St. James, this cute, country French shop sparkles with hand crafted, hand painted goods. Small furnishings, intimate finishing pieces, stenciled hat boxes, framed art fill Mickey Finn's with warmth and charm.

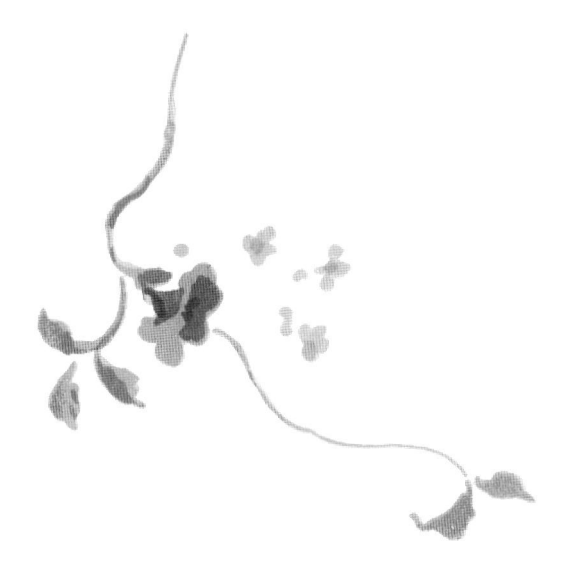

TWIN CITIES SHOPPING MALLS

The shopping mall is a Minnesota invention. Since Southdale opened in 1956, the enclosed mall has been reinvented many times. Although we have not detailed the shops within the malls located in the metro area, a listing of the major malls follows. Once again Minnesota will make retailing history when the quintessential arena of commerce, the Mall of America, opens in Bloomington.

Brookdale
Highway 100 and Brooklyn Boulevard
Brooklyn Center 55430
566-6672

Burnsville Center
35W and County Road 42
Burnsville 55337
435-8181

Eden Prairie Center
494 and 212/169 South
Eden Prairie 55344
941-7650

Maplewood Mall
494 and White Bear Avenue
Maplewood 55109
770-5020

Northtown
Highway 10 and University Avenue N.E.
Blaine 55434
786-9704

Ridgedale
394 and Plymouth Road
Minnetonka 55343
541-4864

Rosedale
West Highway 36 and Fairview Avenue North
Roseville 55113
633-0872

Southdale
France Avenue South and 66th
Edina 55435
925-7885

ABOUT THE AUTHORS . . .

Alison O'Connell brings her fascination and savvy for shopping to this first-of-a-kind guide to the Minneapolis/St. Paul retail market. After executive posts with Estee Lauder, two international airlines, a steamship line and several well-known companies and law firms, Alison has accepted her most challenging assignment -- spreading the good news about what fun shopping is in the Twin Cities. A native Minneapolitan, Alison has resided in Honolulu, London and New York and has had an opportunity to shop in thousands of retail stores around the world. Known as the consumer's connoisseur, Alison has parlayed her shopping strategies into this essential text on powerful and prudent buying.

Ted May, in between international literary and art tours, spends a good portion of his busy executive and volunteer life scouring the retail haunts of Minneapolis and St. Paul. He leaves no stones unturned in his relentless quest for style and value. Ted admits to power shopping and is given to moments of impulse buying. Ted feels -- and rightly so -- that "It matters not <u>where</u> you shop, but <u>how</u>!"

INDEXES

SHOPS BY LOCATION

DOWNTOWN MINNEAPOLIS

Acapulco	51
Albrecht's	39
Ann Klein	20
Ann Taylor	33
Banana Republic	26, 34
Barrie Pace, Ltd.	16
Baxter's Books	22
Beard Galleries	44
Bocce	51
Brentano's Book Store	21
Brit's Pub	45
Brooks Brothers	40
Burberry's of London	17
Cache	20
Cafe Brenda	53
Cafe Solo	54
Call Of The Wild	35
Carson Pirie Scott	24
Charles Couture	37
Charles Footwear	38
Chez Bananas	52
Christensen Mix	29
Coach Store	34
Cole-Haan	17
Complements at the Conservatory	30
Coyote	51
Crabtree & Evelyn	31
Crate and Barrel	41
D'Amico Cucina	52
Dayton's	27
Dome Souvenirs Plus	8
Doubleday Book Shop	31
Douglas-Baker Gallery	48
Dublin Walk	46
Eddie Bauer	18
Eddie Bauer Outlet Store	42
Elegance	47
Facets	29
Faegre's	52
FAO Schwartz	36

Fine Line Music Cafe	53
First Issue	19
Flowers On The Mall	43
Gap Kids	34
Gluek's Brewing Company	51
Goodfellows	36
Gregory's	14
H2O Plus	21
Haskell's and the Big Cheese Company	41
Hello Minnesota	46
Hubert White	23
J. B. Hudson Jewelers	28
International Market Square	49
J. D. Hoyt's	53
j. mcgrath & co	16
Jean Stephen Galleries	30
Jessica McClintock, Inc.	21
Jose's	52
Judi Designs	43
Juster's	9
Lane Bryant	25
Larkspur	49
LaSalle Court	37
Laura Ashley	25
Laurel	20
Liemandt's	97
Lillie Rubin	22
Loon Cafe	52
Manny's	47
Mark Shale	32
Minneapolis Public Library	8
Minneapolis Warehouse District	51
Monte Carlo	53
Morton's of Chicago	14
Mother's Work	26
Museum Company	19
Nature Company	31
Neiman Marcus	13
New French Cafe	52
Nikki's	53
Olds Pendleton Shop	15
Orchestra Hall WAMSO Gift Shop	45
Origami	54

Palomino 39
Perspectives Fine Arts Gallery 43
Petite Sophisticate 26
Pickled Parrot 52
Pier 1 Imports 42
Pottery Barn 32
Riverplace/St. Anthony Main 54
Rodier Paris 22
Rosen's Bar & Grill 52
Runyon's 53
Saks Fifth Avenue 15
Sans Souci Leather & Luggage 19
Scandia Imports 25
Shinders 48
Sims 37, 124
Soldati 38
The Icing 17
The Lenox China Store 16
The Living Room 53
The Map Store 23
The Polo/Ralph Lauren Shop 40
The San Francisco Music Box 18
The Sharper Image 32
Williams-Sonoma 35
St. Croix Shop 33
Tejas 33
Urban Traveler 14
Urban Wildlife 52
Vern Carver 44
Victoria's Secret 25
Waters 53
Westminster Lace 18

DOWNTOWN ST. PAUL
Annie's 65
Baby Grand 72
Benjamin's Restaurant 68
Bibelot Shop 70
Blue & White 66
Breedlove's 67
Broomhouse Street 69
Cafe Latte 63
Carriage Hill Plaza 58

Celebration Designs 73
Ciatti's 62
Cooks of Crocus Hill 69
Creative Kidstuff 71
Cottageware Homestore 72
Depth of Field 68
Frank Murphy 58
Grand Spectacle 64
Hungry Mind Book Store 73
In Vision 67
Kramer Gallery 60
John McLean Company 60
Just Grand 63
Leeann Chin 66
Little Dickens 68
Maggie's Corner 71
Minnesota Seasons 66
Nakashian-O'Neil 58
Needlepoint Allie 71
Odegard Books 64, 185
Odegard Encore Books 65
Old Mexico Shop 63
Paperworks 64
Periwinkle 65
Red Balloon Bookshop 70
Saint Paul Hotel 55
Salisbury Flower Market 67
Sonnie's 59
St. Paul Grill 55
Walter Bradley Shoe Shine 59

UPTOWN
A Fine Romance 76
Bacio 82
Bay Street Shoes 78
Benetton 78
Body Language 81
Border's Book Shop 79
C. P. More 81
Dimitrius 82
doo dah! 80
elements 76
Gabriela's 77

Hollywood High 82
intoto 84
Kitchen Window 79
Latitudes Map and Travel Store 83
Ragstock 83
Roomers Gallery 80
Schlampp's 79
Shoe Zoo 76
Textilis 81
Tom Schmidt Salon 83
Toy Boat 80

EDINA
Accessory Collection 92
Banners To Go 94
Belleson's 87
Burwick 'N Tweed 87
Chico's 88, 124
Durr Ltd. 86
Grethan House 92
J-Michael Galleries 88
McMuffee's Ltd. 91
Periwinkles 90
Rainbow Fine Art Gallery 89
R S V P 87
Shelly's Tall Fashions 93
Shoe Allee 94
Simply Splendid 89
Southdale 95
The Children's General Store 94
The Cottage Sampler 90
The Club Room 91
Tidepool Gallery 90
White Oak Gallery 89
Wild Child 88
Wuollett Bakery 93

GALLERIA
A Pea In The Pod 109
A Touch of Glass 110
Accents 112
Ataz 111
Bellini 111

Bockstruck's	113
Caroll of Paris	110
Cedric's	97
Barnes & Noble	106
D. W. Stewart's	99
epitome	105
Fawbush's	110
Frost & Budd	102
Gabberts Furniture & Design	104
Games by James	113
H.O.B.O.	111
I. B. Diffusion	112
Jonci Petites	102
Joseph of Chicago	98
Kafte	104
len druskin	105
Liemandt's	97
Mainstreet Kids	100
Main Street Outfitters	101
Maternal Instincts	101
Mondi	100
Muggin's Doll House, Inc.	108
My Oh My	108
Nancy Lawrence	98
Pappagollo	106
Polly Berg	112
Rocco Altobelli	107
Schmitt Music Company	106
Shades of Vail	103
Shari Rose, Ltd.	99
Signature	114
t. r. christian	109
The Real Nancy Drew	101
Three Rooms Up	103
Truffles Chocolatier	99
Vie de France	96

WAYZATA

Anderson's China	132
Androli Hair Designers	133, 144
An Elegant Place	119
Bird Feed Store	116
Blanc de Blanc	125

Bob's Shoe Repair 132
Bona Celina 118
Bone Adventure 129
Down In The Valley 117
Emerald Evenings 125
Five Swans 128
Foursome Department Store 131
Gerrings Car Wash 116
Great Reflections 120
Hurricane 124
Jan's of Wayzata 122
Lake Street Papery, Inc. 129
McGlynn's Bakery Outlet Store 130
Memories 119
MJ Galleries 118
Orvis-Gokey 121
Picture This Framed 132
P.O.S.H. 122
P.O.S.H. Pantry 127
Serendipity 120
Side Door 126
Silver Creek Design Studio 121
Ski Hut Sporting Goods 117
The Bookcase 127
The Corner Door 120
The Gold Mine 123
The Traveling Collector 122
The Wayzata Children's Shop 128
Brian Walters, Goldsmith 126
Wayzata Mail Center 123
Wayzata Tea Room 124

DEEPHAVEN
Bumbershute 134
Heritage Clock Shop 136
One More Time 134
Sugarbakers 135
Ultimate Function 135

EXCELSIOR
Androli Hair Designs 133, 144
Antiquity Rose 144
Artworks Art & Frame, Inc. 142

D. B. & Co.	140
Excelsior Mill	138
Frog Island Bookstore	143
Gray Gardens	141
Heritage II	144
Kidding Around	141
Kuempel Custom Clockmakers & Repair	145
Mary Ellen Bartholow	143
Mary O'Neal & Co.	142
Once Upon A Time	140
Provisions	138
The Doll Buggy	143
The Sampler	139
The Sign of the Eagle	139
Water Street Clothing Co.	142

ART GALLERIES/MUSEUMS

American Swedish Institute	147
C. G. Rein Galleries	148
Children's Museum	147
elayne	149
Dolly Fiterman Fine Arts	148
Minneapolis Institute of Arts	150
Minnesota Museum of Art	147
Science Museum of Minnesota	148
The Guthrie Theater	149
The Walker Art Center Book Shop	150

ANTIQUES

Aladdin's Antique Alley	162
American Classics Antiques	157
Antique Corner	157
Antiques at our House	157
Antiques Minnesota	156
Architectural Antiques	153
Bill Brantner's Cobblestone Antiques	155
Capitol Arts & Antiques	161
Carrol Shepherd's Consignment Shop	168
Cobweb Antiques	152
Compliments	159
Country School House Shops	166
Deephaven Antiques	169
Early Times Emporium	165

Emporium Antiques	164
Eydie's Country Quilting Shop	158
Fjelde & Co. Antiques	158
Fraser Cameron	167
French Antiques	162
Golden Lion Antiques	164
Gray's Bay Antiques	167
Great River	151
H & B Gallery	154
Hagen's Furniture and Antiques	198
J & E Antiques	165
John's Antiques	163
Lyndale House Antiques /Antiques Wholesale	154
Mainstreet Antique Mall	160
Park Avenue Antiques	157
Payne Avenue Antique Mall	163
Steeple Antiques	166
The Loft	158
Treasures Antique Mall	160
Uptown Mall Antiques	155
Yankee Peddler	159
Yesteryears Appraisal Services	158

CONSIGNMENT SHOPS

Designer Wardrobe	171
Elsie's Closet	172
Encore	172
Repeat Performance	173
Rodeo Drive	174
The Pink Closet	173
Zelda Z's	174

OFF-THE-BEATEN-PATH

Applause	186
Bachman's	26, 181
Bookdale's	184
Bubbles & Scents	191
Byerly's	175
Calamity Jeanne's	193
Century Studios	188
Cossetta	177
Josef's Art Glass/Joe Diethelm	189
Dundee Nursery	181

El Burrito Marquet	177
Energy	190
Farmer's Markets	179
Fiori	180
Gaytee Stained Glass, Inc.	189
Hagen's Furniture and Antiques	198
Half Price Books	184
Hoigaard's	190
Hold It!	194
Homestead Pickin' Parlor	187
Hudson Map Company	192
Ingebretsen's Scandinavian Center	178
Josef's Art Glass/Joe Diethelm	189
Litin Paper Company	192
Lund's	176
Lyndale Garden Center	182
Judith McGrann & Friends	196
Milano's	178
Mill End Textiles	197
Minnesota Landscape Arboretum	183
Musicland	188
Odegard Books	64, 185
Old America Store	196
Once Upon A Crime	185
Orvis-Gokey	121
Otten Brothers Nursery	182
Planes of Fame	198
Plastic Bag Mart	195
Schatzlein Saddle Shop	193
Steve Hoag's Marathon Sports	191
The Electric Fetus	187
The General Store of Minnetonka	197
The Lincoln Del	180
Two's Company	195
Uncle Hugo's Science Fiction Bookstore	186
Wagner Greenhouse	183
Wicker Works	194

SERVICES

Aero Custom Window Fashions	204
Anderson's Lampshades	207
Anthony's Furniture Restoration	199
Apres, Inc.	207

Arch Books 205
China & Crystal Replacements 200
Dale Services 208
Darling Drapery and Carpet Cleaning 203
Mary Elizabeth Draperies 203
John Fox Chair Caning 199
Invisible China Repair and Restoration 200
Gerald Ludwig Art Work Repair 201
Michael's Lamp Studio 206
Minnesota State Button Society 206
Mr. & Mrs. Chips 201
Oexning Silversmiths 202
Vale Typewriter Repair 208
Valley Clockworks 202
Wizard Weavers 205

BY APPOINTMENT ONLY
Amundson and McDonald Photography 209
Barbara Lund Photography 210
Bellezza 213
Big Kids, Inc. 213
Bravo Bras 211
D. Dawley & Co. 211
Daniel's Animal Portrait 209
Doncaster/Gai Skramstad 212
Estee Lauder Spas at Dayton's Southdale 214
Gianneti Photography 210
Leonard Dixon/Gallery West Photography 210
Mary Kay Cosmetics 215
The Carlisle Collection, Ltd. 212
The Day Spa 214
The Marsh 215
Victorian Treasures 216

INDEX BY STORE/SERVICE TYPE

DEPARTMENT STORES
Carson Pirie Scott 24
Dayton's 27
Neiman Marcus 13
Saks Fifth Avenue 15

JEWELRY, FINE CHINA & CRYSTAL
A Touch of Glass 110
Anderson's China 132
Bockstrucks's 113
Dublin Walk 46
Facets 29
J. B. Hudson Jewelers 28
The Lenox China Store 16
t. r. christian 109
Brian L. Walters, Goldsmith 126

CARDS, GIFTS, DECORATIVE ITEMS
A Fine Romance 76
Accessory Collection 92
An Elegant Place 119
Blanc de Blanc 125
Blue & White 66
Broomhouse Street 69
Call of the Wild 35
Celebration Designs 73
D.B. & Company 140
doo dah! 80
Five Swans 128
Frost & Budd 102
Hello Minnesota 46
j. mcgrath 16
Just Grand 63
Lake Street Papery, Inc. 129
Litin Paper Company 192
Minnesota Seasons 66
My Oh My 108
Old Mexico Shop 63
Paperworks 64
Periwinkle 65

Periwinkles	90
Plastic Bag Mart	195
Provisions	138
RSVP	87
Scandia Imports	25
Simply Splendid	89
The Bibelot Shop	70
The Cottage Sampler	90
The General Store of Minnetonka	197
The Museum Company	19
The Nature Company	31
The Real Nancy Drew	101
The San Francisco Music Box Company	18
The Sharper Image	32
The Traveling Collector	122
Two's Company	195
Signature	114
Ultimate Function	135

MEN'S AND WOMEN'S CLOTHING

Aeropostale	26
Banana Republic	34
Brooks Brothers	40
Burberry's of London	17
Burwick 'N Tweed	87
Cedric's	97
County Seat	25
Eddie Bauer	18
Eddie Bauer Outlet	42
Elegance	47
Foursome Department Store	131
Hurricane	124
intoto	84
Juster's	9
Liemandt's	97
Mainstreet Outfitters	101
Mark Shale	32
Olds Pendleton	15
Orvis-Gokey	121
Polo/Ralph Loren	40
Ragstock	33

WOMEN'S CLOTHING

Albrecht's	39
Ann Taylor	33
Anne Klein	20
Annie's	65
Barrie Pace	16
Benetton	78
Breedlove's	67
Cache	20
Caroll of Paris	110
Chico's	88, 124
epitome	105
Fawbush's	110
First Issue	19
Frank Murphy	58
Gantos	26
Grethan House	92
H.O.B.O.	111
Hollywood High	82
I. B. Diffusion	112
Jan's of Wayzata	122
Jessica McClintock	21
Laura Ashley	25
Laurel	20
len druskin	105
Lillie Rubin	22
Limited	25
Limited Express	25
McMuffee's	91
Mondi	100
Rodier Paris	22
Schlampp's	79
Sonnie's	59
Talbots	124
The Side Door	126
Water Street Clothing	142

SPECIALTY CLOTHING
PETITES

Jonci	102
Petite Sophisticate	26

TALL
D. W. Stewart's (Men) 99
Shelly's Tall Fashions 93

LARGE SIZES
Lane Bryant 25
Nancy Lawrence 98

EQUESTRIAN
Calamity Jeanne's 193
Schatzlein Saddle Shop 193

LINGERIE
Polly Berg 112
Victoria's Secret 25

MATERNITY
A Pea In The Pod 109
Maternal Instincts 101
Mother's Work 26

ACCESSORIES
Accents 112
C. P. More 81
Complements at the Conservatory 30
The Coach Store 34
The Icing 17
Sans Souci Leather & Luggage 19

SHOES
Bay Street Shoes 78
Charles Footwear 38
Cole Haan 17
Foot Locker 23
Foursome Department Store 131
Gregory's 14
Joseph of Chicago 98
Pappagallo 106
Shoe Allee 94
Soldati 38

MEN'S APPAREL
Bacio 82
Belleson's 87
Charles Couture 37
Christensen Mix Ltd 29
D. W. Stewart's 99

Dimitrius 82
D. W. Stewart's 23
Hubert W. White 97
Sims, Ltd. 37, 124
St. Croix Shop 33

VINTAGE & CONSIGNMENT CLOTHING
Bona Celina 118
Designer Wardrobe 171
Elsie's Closet 172
Emerald Evenings 125
Encore 172
Gabriela's 77
Repeat Performance 173
Rodeo Drive 174
The Pink Closet 173
Zelda Z's 174

CHILDREN'S CLOTHING & ACCESSORIES
Baby Grand 72
Bellini 111
Creative Kidstuff 71
FAO Schwarz 36
Foursome Department Store 131
Gap Kids 34
Kidding Around 141
Little Dickens 68
Mainstreet Kids 100
Muggins Doll House, Inc. 108
One More Time 134
Serendipity 120
Shoe Zoo 76
The Children's General Store 94
The Doll Buggy 143
Toy Boat 80
Wayzata Children's Store 128
Wild Child 88

HEALTH & BEAUTY
Androli Hair Designs 133, 144
Bellezza 213
Big Kids, Inc. 213
Bubbles & Scents 191

Crabtree & Evelyn 31
Estee Lauder Spa at Dayton's Southdale 214
H2O Plus 21
Mary Kay Cosmetics 215
Rocco Altobelli 107
Rodica Facial Salon 124
Salon Marquee 124
The Day Spa 214
The Marsh 215
Tom Schmidt Salon 83

FLOWERS & NURSERIES
Bachman's 26, 181
Dundee Nursery 181
Fiori 180
Flowers On The Mall 43
Gray Gardens 141
Judi Designs 43
Larkspur 49
Lyndale Garden Center 182
Otten Brothers Nursery 182
Salisbury Flower Market 67
Wagner Greenhouse 183

HOME FURNISHINGS
Aero Custom Window Fashions 204
Anderson's Lampshades 207
Century Studios 188
Cottageware Homestore 72
Crate & Barrel 41
Durr Ltd. 86
Elements 76
Gabberts Furniture & Design 104
Gaytee Stained Glass, Inc. 189
Heritage II 144
Heritage Clock Shop 136
Hoigaard's 190
Hold It! 114
Josef's Art Glass/Joe Diethelm 189
Mary Elizabeth Draperies 203
Michael's Lamp Studio 206
Old America Store 196
Pier 1 42

P.O.S.H. 122
Pottery Barn 32
Shari Rose, Ltd. 99
Silver Creek Design Studio 121
Sugarbakers 135
Textilis 81
The Sign of the Eagle 139
Westminster Lace 18
Wicker Works 194

KITCHEN WARES
Cooks of Crocus Hill 69
Hoffritz 26
Kitchen Window 79
P.O.S.H. Pantry 127
Provisions 138
Williams Sonoma 35

THE ARTS AND MUSEUMS
American Swedish Institute 147
Ataz 110
Beard Galleris 44
C. G. Rein Galleries 148
Children's Museum 147
Dolly Fiterman Fine Arts 148
elayne 149
J-Michael Galleries 88
Jean Stephen Galleries 30
Kramer Gallery 60
Minneapolis Institute of Arts 150
Minneapolis Public Library 8
Minnesota Landscape Arboretum 183
Minnesota Museum of Art 147
MJ Galleries 118
Orchestra Hall WAMSO Gift Shop 45
Perspectives Fine Art Gallery 43
Planes of Fame 198
Rainbow Fine Art Gallery 89
Roomers Gallery 80
Science Museum of Minnesota 148
The Douglas Baker Gallery 48
The Guthrie Theater 149
The Walker Art Center 150

Three Rooms Up 103
Tidepool Gallery 90
Vern Carver Gallery 44
White Oak Gallery 89

ANTIQUES
Aladdin's Antique Alley 162
American Classics Antiques 157
Antiques At Our House 157
Antiques Minnesota 156
Antiquity Rose 144
Architectural Antiques 152
Bill Brantner's Cobblestone Antiques 155
Capitol Arts and Antiques 161
Carrol Shepherd's Consignment Shop 168
Cobweb Antiques 152
Complimetns 159
Country School House Shops 166
Deephaven Antiques 168
Early Times Emporium 165
Emporium Antiques 164
Fjelde & Co. Antiques 158
Fraser Cameron 167
French Antiques 162
Golden Lion Antiques 164
Gray's Bay Antiques 167
Great River Antiques 151
H & B Gallery 154
Hagen's Furniture & Antiques 198
J & E Antiques 165
John's Antiques 163
Lyndale House Antiques 153
Maggie's Corner 71
Mainstreet Antique Mall 160
Mary O'Neal & Co. 142
Memories 119
Nakashian-O'Neil 58
Once Upon A Time 140
Park Avenue Antiques 157
Payne Avenue Antique Mall 163
Steeple Antiques 166
The Corner Door 120
The Gold Mine 123

The Loft	158
Treasures Antiques	160
Uptown Mall Antiques	155
Yankee Peddler	159
Yesteryears Appraisal Services	158

HOBBY/LEISURE

Bird Feed Store	116
Body Language	81
Bone Adventure	129
Depth of Field	68
Dome Souvenirs	8
Energy	190
Eydie's Country Quilting Shop	158
Games by James	113
Hudson Map Company	192
Latitudes Map & Travel Store	82
Mill End Textiles	196
Minnesota State Button Society	206
Needlepoint Allie	71
Ski Hut Sporting Goods	117
Steve Hoag's Marathon Sports	191
The Club Room	91
The Map Store	23
The Sampler	139
Urban Traveler	14

BOOKS

Arch Books	205
B. Dalton Bookstore	26
Barnes & Noble	106
Baxter's Books	22
Bookdales	184
Borders Book Shop	79
Brentano's Book Store	21
Doubleday Book Shop	31
Frog Island Bookstore	143
Half Price Books	184
Hungry Mind Book Store	73
Odegard Books	64, 185
Odegar Encore Books	65
Once Upon A Crime	185
Shinders	48

The Bookcase 127
The Red Balloon Bookshop 69
Uncle Hugo's Science Fiction Bookstore 186

MUSIC
Applause 186
Down In The Valley 117
Homestead Pickin' Parlor 187
Musicland 188
Schmitt Music Company 106
The Electric Fetus 187

OPTICAL
Christy Optical 59
Grand Spectacle 64
In Vision 67
Latham Optical 124
Northwest Opticians 59
Shades of Vail 102

BY APPOINTMENT
Amundson and McDonald Photography 209
Barbara Lund Photography 210
Bravo Bras 211
D. Dawley & Co. 211
Daniels Animal Portraits 209
Doncaster 211
Gianneti Photography 210
Leonard Dixon Photography 210
The Carlisle Collection 212
Victorian Treasures 216

SERVICES
Anthony's Furniture Restoration 199
Antique Clock Repair 157
Apres 207
Artworks Art & Frame, Inc. 141
Banners To Go 94
Bob's Shoe Repair 132
China & Crystal Replacements 200
Dale Services 208
Darling Drapery 203
Gerald Ludwig Art Work Repair 201

Gerrings Car Wash 116
Great Reflections 120
Invisible China Repair & Restoration 200
John Fox Chair Caning 199
Kuemple Custom Clockmakers & Repair 145
Mary Ellen Bartholow 143
Mr. & Mrs. Chipos 201
Oexning Silversmiths 202
Picture This Framed 132
The Lampmender 157
Vale Typewriter Repair 208
Valley Clockworks 202
Walter Bradley Shoeshine 59
Wayzata Mail Center 123
Wizard Weavers 205

EDIBLES
Acapulco 51
Benjamins 68
Blue Point 115
Bocce 51
Brit's Pub 45
Byerly's 175
Cafe Brenda 53
Cafe Latte 63
Cafe Solo 54
Chez Bananas 52
Ciatti's 62
Cossetta 177
Coyote 51
D'Amico Cucina 51
Ediner 96
El Burrito Marquet 177
Faegre's 52
Farmer's Markets 179
Fine Line Music Cafe 52
Gloria Jean's 26
Gluek's Brewing Company 51
Good Earth 96
Goodfellows 36
Haskell's and The Big Cheese Company 41
Hunter's Glen 129
Ingebretsen's Scandinavian Center 178

J. D. Hoyt's	53
John McLean & Co.	60
Jose's	52
Kafte	103
Leeann Chin	66
Loon Cafe	52
Lunds	176
Manny's	47
McGlynn's Bakery Outlet Store	130
Mitano's	178
Monte Carlo	53
Morton's of Chicago	14
New French Cafe	52
Nikki's	53
Origami	53
Palomino	39
Pickled Parrot	52
Rosebud Grocery	96
Runyon's	53
Sasha's	115
St. Paul Hotel Grill	55
Sunsets	115
Tejas	33
The Lincoln Del	180
The Living Room	53
Truffles Chocolatier	99
Urban Wildlife	52
Vie de France	96
Water's	53
Wayzata Tea Room	124
Woullet Bakery	93

DAY TRIPS
Stillwater/Afton	217
Hastings/Red Wing	231

ALPHABETICAL INDEX

A Fine Romance 76
A Pea In The Pod 109
A Touch of Glass 110
Acapulco 51
Accents 112
Accessory Collection 92
Aero Custom Window Fashions 204
Aeropostale 26
Aladdin's Antique Alley 162
Albrecht's 39
American Classics Antiques 157
American Swedish Institute 147
Amundson and McDonald Photography 209
An Elegant Place 119
Anderson's China 132
Anderson's Lampshades 207
Androli Hair Designers 133, 144
Ann Taylor 33
Anne Klein 20
Annie's 65
Anthony's Furniture Restoration 199
Antique Clock Repair 155
Antique Corner 157
Antiques at Our House 157
Antiques Minnesota 156
Antiquity Rose 144
Applause 186
Apres, Inc. 207
Arch Books 205
Architectural Antiques 153
Artworks Art & Frame, Inc. 142
Ataz 111
B. Dalton Bookstore 26
Baby Grand 72
Bachman's 26, 181
Bacio 82
Banana Republic 26, 34
Banners To Go 94
Barbara Lund Photography 210
Barnes & Noble 106
Barrie Pace Ltd. 16

Baxter's Books	22
Bay Street Shoes	78
Beard Galleries	44
Belleson's	87
Bellezza	213
Bellini	111
Benetton	78
Benjamin's Restaurant	68
Big Kids, Inc.	213
Bill Brantner's Cobblestone Antiques	155
Bird Feed Store	116
Blanc de Blanc	125
Blue and White	66
Blue Point	115
Bob's Shoe Repair	132
Bocce	51
Bockstruck's	113
Body Language	81
Bona Celina	118
Bone Adventure	129
Bookdales	184
Borders Book Shop	79
Bravo Bras	211
Breedlove's	67
Brentano's Book Store	21
Brit's Pub	45
Brooks Brothers	40
Broomhouse Street	69
Bubbles & Scents	191
Bumbershute	134
Burberrys of London	17
Burwick 'N Tweed	87
Byerly's	175
C. G. Rein Galleries	148
C. P. More	81
Cache	20
Cafe Brenda	53
Cafe Latte	63
Cafe Solo	54
Calamity Jeanne's	193
Call of the Wild	35
Capitol Arts & Antiques	161
Caroll of Paris	110

Carrol Shepherd's Consignment Shop 168
Carson Pirie Scott 24
Cedric's 97
Celebration Designs 73
Century Studios 188
Charles Couture 37
Charles Footwear 38
Chez Bananas 52
Chico's 88, 124
Children's Museum 147
China and Crystal Replacements 200
Christensen Mix Ltd. 29
Christy Optical 59
Ciatti's 62
Cobweb Antiques 152
Cole-Haan 17
Complements at the Conservatory 30
Compliments 159
Cooks of Crocus Hill 69
Cossetta 177
Cottageware Homestore 72
Country School House Shops 166
County Seat 25
Coyote 51
Crabtree & Evelyn 31
Crate and Barrel 41
Creative Kidstuff 71
D. Dawley & Co. 211
D. W. Stewart's 99
D.B. & Company 140
D'Amico Cucina 52
Dale Services 208
Daniels Animal Portraits 209
Darling Drapery and Carpet Cleaning 203
Dayton's 27
Deephaven 134
Deephaven Antiques 169
Depth of Field 68
Designer Wardrobe 171
Dimitrius 82
Dolly Fiterman Fine Arts 148
Dome Souvenirs Plus 8
Doncaster 212

doo dah!	80
Doubleday Book Shop	31
Down in the Valley	117
Dublin Walk	46
Dundee Nursery	181
Durr Ltd.	86
Early Times Emporium	165
Eddie Bauer	18
Eddie Bauer Outlet Store	42
Edina	85
Ediner	96
El Burrito Marquet	177
elayne	149
Elegance	47
Elements	76
Elsie's Closet	172
Emerald Evenings	125
Emporium Antiques	164
Encore	172
Energy	190
epitome	105
Estee Lauder Spa at Dayton's Southdale	214
Excelsior Mill	138
Eydie's Country Quilting Shop	158
Facets	29
Faegre's	52
FAO Schwarz	36
Farmers' Market	179
Fawbush's	110
Fine Line Music Cafe	53
Fiori	180
First Issue	19
Five Swans	128
Fjelde & Co. Antiques	158
Flowers On The Mall	43
Foot Locker	25
Foursome Department Store	131
Frank Murphy	58
Fraser Cameron	167
French Antiques	162
Frog Island Bookstore	143
Frost & Budd	102
Gabberts Furniture & Design	104

Gabriela's	77
Games by James	113
Gantos	26
Gap Kids	34
Gaviidae Common	11
Gaytee Stained Glass, Inc.	189
Gerald Ludwig Art Work Repair	201
Gerrings Car Wash	116
Gianneti Photography	210
Gloria Jean's	26
Gluek's Brewing Company	51
Golden Lion Antiques	164
Good Earth	96
Goodfellows	36
Grand Avenue	61
Grand Spectacle	64
Gray Gardens	141
Gray's Bay Antiques	167
Great Reflections	120
Great River Antiques	151
Gregory's	14
Grethan House	92
H & B Gallery	154
H.O.B.O.	111
H2O Plus	21
Hagen's Furniture and Antiques	198
Half Price Books	184
Haskell's and The Big Cheese Company	41
Hello Minnesota	46
Heritage II	144
Heritage Clock Shop	136
Hoffritz	26
Hoigaard's	190
Hold It!	194
Hollywood High	82
Homestead Pickin' Parlor	187
Hubert W. White	23
Hudson Map Company	192
Hungry Mind Book Store	73
Hunter's Glen	129
Hurricane	124
I. B. Diffusion	112
In Vision	67

Ingebretsen's Scandinavian Center	178
intoto	84
Invisible China Repair and Restoration	200
J & E Antiques	165
J. B. Hudson Jewelers	28
J. D. Hoyt's	53
j. mcgrath & co.	16
J-Michael Galleries	88
Jan's of Wayzata	122
Jean Stephen Galleries	30
Jessica McClintock, Inc.	21
John Fox Chair Caning	199
John McLean Company	60
John's Antiques	163
Jonci Petites	102
Jose's	52
Josef's Art Glass/Joe Diethelm	189
Joseph of Chicago	98
Judi Designs	43
Just Grand	63
Juster's	9
Kafte	104
Kidding Around	141
Kitchen Window	79
Kramer Gallery	60
Kuempel Custom Clockmakers and Repair	145
Lake Street Papery, Inc.	129
Lane Bryant	25
Larkspur	49
Latham Optical	124
Latitudes Map and Travel Store	83
Laura Ashley	25
Laurel	20
Leeann Chin	66
len druskin	105
Leonard Dixon Gallery West Photography	210
Liemandt's	97
Lillie Rubin	22
Limited	25
Limited Express	25
Litin Paper Company	192
Little Dickens	68
Loon Cafe	52

Lunds 176
Lyndale Garden Center 182
Lyndale House Antiques/Antiques Wholesale 154
Maggie's Corner 71
Main Street Outfitters 101
Mainstreet Antique Mall 160
MainStreet Kids 100
Manny's 47
Mark Shale 32
Mary Elizabeth Draperies 203
Mary Ellen Bartholow 143
Mary Kay Cosmetics 215
Mary O'Neal & Co. 142
Maternal Instincts 101
McGlynn's Bakery Outlet Store 130
McMuffee's Ltd. 91
Memories 119
Michael's Lamp Studio 206
Milano's 178
Mill End Textiles 197
Minneapolis Institute of Arts 150
Minneapolis Public Library 8
Minnesota Landscape Arboretum 183
Minnesota Museum of Art 147
Minnesota Public Radio 4
Minnesota Seasons 66
Minnesota State Button Society 206
MJ Galleries 118
Mondi 100
Monte Carlo 53
Morton's of Chicago 14
Mother's Work 26
Mr. & Mrs. Chips 201
Muggins Doll House, Inc. 108
Musicland 188
My Oh My 108
Nakashian-O'Neil 58
Nancy Lawrence 98
Needlepoint Allie 71
Neiman Marcus 13
New French Cafe 52
Nikki's 53
Northwest Opticians 59

Odegard Books	64, 185
Odegard Encore Books	65
Oexning Silversmiths	202
Old America Store	196
Old Mexico Shop, Inc.	63
Olds Pendleton Shop	15
Once Upon A Crime	185
Once Upon A Time	140
One More Time	134
Orchestra Hall WAMSO Gift Shop	45
Origami	54
Orvis-Gokey	121
Otten Brothers Nursery	182
P.O.S.H.	122
P.O.S.H. Pantry	127
Palomino	39
Paperworks	64
Pappagallo	106
Park Avenue Antiques	157
Payne Avenue Antique Mall	163
Periwinkle	65
Periwinkles	90
Perspectives Fine Arts Gallery	43
Petite Sophisticate	26
Pickled Parrot	52
Picture This Framed	132
Pier 1 Imports	42
Planes of Fame	198
Plastic Bag Mart	195
Polly Berg	112
Pottery Barn	32
Provisions	138
R S V P	87
Ragstock	83
Rainbow Fine Art Gallery	89
Red Wing	234
Repeat Performance	173
Rocco Altobelli	107
Rodeo Drive	174
Rodica Facial Salon	124
Rodier Paris	22
Roomers Gallery	80
Rosebud Grocery	96

Rosen's Bar & Grill 52
Runyon's 53
Saks Fifth Avenue 15
Salisbury Flower Market 67
Salon Marquee 124
Sans Souci Leather & Luggage 19
Sasha's 115
Scandia Imports 25
Schatzlein Saddle Shop 193
Schlampp's 79
Schmitt Music Company 107
Science Museum of Minnesota 148
Serendipity 120
Shades of Vail 103
Shari Rose, Ltd. 99
Shelly's Tall Fashions 93
Shinder's 48
Shoe Allee 94
Shoe Zoo 76
Signature 114
Silver Creek Design Studio 121
Simply Splendid 89
Sims 37, 124
Ski Hut Sporting Goods 117
Soldati 38
Sonnie's 59
St. Croix Shop 33
St. Paul Grill 55
Steeple Antiques 166
Steve Hoag's Marathon Sports 191
Sugarbakers 135
Sunsets 115
t. r. christian 109
Talbots 124
Tejas 33
Textilis 81
The Bibelot Shop 70
The Bookcase 127
The Carlisle Collection, LTD. 212
The Children's General Store 94
The Club Room 91
The Coach Store 34
The Corner Door 120

The Cottage Sampler 90
The Day Spa 214
The Doll Buggy 143
The Douglas-Baker Gallery 48
The Electric Fetus 187
The General Store of Minnetonka 197
The Gold Mine 123
The Guthrie Theater 149
The Icing 17
The Lampmender 156
The Lenox China Store 16
The Lincoln Del 180
The Living Room 53
The Loft 158
The Map Store 23
The Marsh 215
The Museum Company 19
The Nature Company 31
The Pink Closet 173
The Polo/Ralph Lauren Shop 40
The Real Nancy Drew 101
The Red Balloon Bookshop 70
The Sampler 139
The San Francisco Music Box Company 18
The Sharper Image 32
The Side Door 126
The Sign of the Eagle 139
The Traveling Collector 122
The Walker Art Center Book Shop 150
The Wayzata Children's Shop 128
Three Rooms Up 103
Ticketmaster 5
Tidepool Gallery 90
Tom Schmidt Salon 83
Toy Boat 80
Treasures Antique Mall 160
Truffles Chocolatier 99
Two's Company 195
Ultimate Function 135
Uncle Hugo's Science Fiction Bookstore 186
Uptown Mall Antiques 155
Urban Traveler 14
Urban Wildlife 52

Vale Typewriter Repair 208
Valley Clockworks 202
Vern Carver Gallery 44
Victoria's Secret 25
Victorian Treasures 216
Vie de France 96
Wagner Greenhouse 183
Brian L. Walters, Goldsmith 126
Water Street Clothing Co. 142
Water's 53
Wayzata Mail Center 123
Wayzata Marquee Place 124
Wayzata Tea Room 124
Westminster Lace 18
White Oak Gallery 89
Wicker Works 194
Wild Child 88
Williams-Sonoma 35
Wizard Weavers 205
Wuollet Bakery 93
Yankee Peddler 159
Yesteryears Appraisal Services 158
Zelda Z's 174

ORDER FORM

SHOPPING THE TWIN CITIES... and more is selling like hotcakes and may be out of stock at your local retailer. Copies are available from the publisher at a cost of $12.95 each plus 6.5% Sales Tax, for a total of $13.79. Please add $2.00 shipping and handling charge for each book. No shipping/handling charge on orders of ten books or more.

____ Books @ $12.95 .... $_____

6.5% Sales Tax .... $_____

If less than 10 books
Shipping/Handling
Charge @ $2.00 x ____ Books .... $_____

TOTAL ORDER .... $_____

NAME: _____

ADDRESS: _____

CITY: _____ STATE _____ ZIP _____

Please mail this form with your check to:

CHAMBERLIN PUBLISHING
Suite 700
3300 Edinborough Way
Edina, MN 55435